DESPERATELY SEEKING SALVATION

Shalom Blessings
Joe !

T J Guthrie

DESPERATELY SEEKING SALVATION

Prophetic Scriptures from the Law of Moses,
the Prophets and the Psalms

DR. JANIEL GUTHRIE

DESPERATELY SEEKING SALVATION

© 2012 by Janiel Guthrie

TrueNorth Ink (www.truenorthpublish.com)

ISBN 978-1480194069

Published in the United States of America. For worldwide distribution.

"You search the Scriptures, for in them you think you have Eternal Life; and these are they which testify of Me." - *Yochanan (John) 5:39 NKJV*

But you, O Daniel, shut up the words and seal the Book until the time of the end. [Then] many shall run to and fro and search anxiously [through the Book], and knowledge [of God's purposes as revealed by His prophets] shall be increased and become great. - *Daniel 12:4*

Contents

THE PROPHETS

SALVATION: MEANING OF THE WORD IN HEBREW FROM THE HOLY SCRIPTURES

*3444 Yeshuw`ah, yesh-oo'aw; something saved, deliverance; hence, aid, victory, prosperity:--deliverance, health, help(-ing), salvation, save, saving (health), welfare.

Phonetically, this word is Yeshua (endnote 1)

PURPOSE

The loving purpose of this book is to present a compilation of the Messianic prophecies from the Holy Scriptures and their fulfillments. In the Hebrew culture, God's Word is called the Tanakh (Old Testament) and the B'rit Hadashah (New Testament). The prophecies are between 500 to more than 1,200 years before Yeshua (Jesus) Messiah (Christ, the Anointed One) was born.

The Scriptures (unless otherwise noted) are from the Amplified version of the Holy Bible. This version expounds the meaning of the words from the original Hebrew and Greek.

Father God Almighty, I dedicate this work to You and ask You to lead and guide me and compile it through me by Your Ruach Ha'Kodesh (Holy Spirit) so that many eyes shall be opened, and many souls shall be saved; for Your glory; in Yeshua's (Jesus') Name, Amen (so be it).

Janiel Guthrie, PhD

Then He said to them: "These are the words which I spoke to you while I was still with you, that all things must be fulfilled which were written in the Law of Moses and the Prophets and the Psalms concerning Me." - *(Yeshua) Jesus*

And He opened their understanding, that they might comprehend the Scriptures. - *Luke 24:44-45 NKJV*

DEDICATION

To my precious Holy One; the Beloved of my soul: Yeshua (Salvation).

"Then the LORD answered me and said: "Write the vision and make it plain on tablets, that he may run who reads it." - *Habakkuk 2:2*

A NEW COVENANT

Yet He has made with me an everlasting covenant, ordered in all things and secure. For this is all my Salvation and all my desire; will He not make it increase? - *2 Samuel 23:5 NKJV*

Behold, the days come, says the LORD, that I will make A NEW COVENANT with the house of Israel, and with the house of Judah.
- *Jeremiah 31:31 NKJV*

This cup is the New Covenant in My Blood, which is shed for you.
- *Yeshua (Jesus) in Luke 22:20*

[Christ, the Messiah] is therefore the Negotiator and Mediator of an [entirely] new agreement (testament, covenant), so that those who are called and offered it may receive the fulfillment of the promised everlasting inheritance--since a death has taken place which rescues and delivers and redeems them from the transgressions committed under the [old] first agreement. - *Hebrews 9:14-15*

Throughout history, many wrongs have been done to the Jewish people by unscrupulous persons in the name of religion; even in the name of Christ. I humbly declare that this was an attempt by the enemy of their souls (the devil) to try to abort their salvation and destiny. Yeshua (Jesus) Himself even said many would come in His name, but would be false (Matthew 24). He also said you would know people by the fruit that came from their lives. Good fruit - good tree; bad fruit - bad tree. Nobody took Jesus' life. He laid down His life for us in the perfect plan of Salvation. Let us take our eyes off mankind, and look to the Rock from which we were hewn.

Books of Moses

GENESIS: In the Beginning ... GOD

IN THE beginning GOD (prepared, formed, fashioned, and) created the heavens and the earth.

The earth was without form and an empty waste, and darkness was upon the face of the very great deep. The Spirit of God was moving (hovering, brooding) over the face of the waters.

And GOD SAID, Let there be light; and there was light. - *Genesis 1:1-3*

NEW COVENANT REFERENCES

IN THE beginning [before all time] was the Word (Christ), and the Word was with God, and the Word was God Himself.

He was present originally with God.

All things were made and came into existence through Him; and without Him was not even one thing made that has come into being.

In Him was Life, and the Life was the Light of men. - *Yochanan (John) 1:1-4*

He came into the world, and though the world was made through Him, the world did not recognize Him [did not know Him].

He came to that which belonged to Him [to His own--His domain, creation, things, world], and they who were His own did not receive Him and did not welcome Him.

But to as many as did receive and welcome Him, He gave the authority (power, privilege, right) to become the children of God, that is to those who believe in (adhere to, trust in, and rely on) His name. - *Yochanan (John) 1:10-12*

And the Word (Christ) became flesh (human, incarnate) and tabernacled (fixed His tent of flesh, lived awhile) among us; and we [actually] saw His glory (His honor, His majesty), such glory as an only begotten Son receives from His Father, full of grace (favor, loving-kindness) and Truth. - *Yochanan (John) 1:14*

GOD spoke the creation into existence. In Yochanan (John) 1:1, He is called The Word. He became flesh in order to be the Lamb of God Who takes away the sins of the world. This is the New Covenant. He gave His life as the Lamb of God to Atone for our sins. This book presents the Biblical prophecies and their fulfillments by Yeshua (Jesus) the Messiah (the Christ, the Anointed One). Yeshua means "Salvation."

GENESIS: Sin and Atonement, Both Began in a Garden

And the LORD God commanded the man, saying, Of every tree of the garden you may freely eat: But of the tree of the knowledge of good and evil, you shall not eat of it: for in the day that you eat of it, you shall surely die. - *Genesis 2:16-17 KJV*

When Adam and Eve disobeyed God in the garden of Eden, sin began upon the earth. When Yeshua (Jesus) went to the Garden of Gethsemane to pray before His arrest, He sweated great drops of blood. His Blood was shed for our atonement, and His agony began in a garden. Gethsemane means "Olive Press."

NEW COVENANT REFERENCES

Then Jesus went with them to a place called Gethsemane, and He told His disciples, Sit down here while I go over yonder and pray... Then He said to them, My soul is very sad and deeply grieved, so that I am almost dying of sorrow... - *Matthew 26:36, 38a*

And He took with Him Peter and James and John, and began to be struck with terror and amazement and deeply troubled and depressed. And He said to them, My soul is exceedingly sad (overwhelmed with grief) so that it almost kills Me! - *Mark 14:33-34a*

And being in an agony He prayed more earnestly: and His sweat was as it were great drops of blood falling down to the ground. - *Luke 22:44 KJV*

GENESIS: God is Triune, Three-in-One

And God said, Let Us make man in Our image, after Our likeness.
- *Genesis 1:26*

Mankind (male and female) created in God's image is a triune being: having a spirit, a soul (mind, emotions and will) and a physical body.

1. And the LORD appeared to him (Abraham) in the plains of Mamre: and he sat in the tent door in the heat of the day;

2. And he lifted up his eyes and looked, and, behold, three Men stood by him: and when he saw Them, he ran to meet Them from the tent door, and bowed himself toward the ground,

3. And said, My LORD, if now I have found favor in Your sight, pass not away, I pray You, from Your servant. - *Genesis 18:1-3*

It is interesting to note that the Scriptures in Genesis 18 that show the LORD as a Triune Being are in verses 1, 2 and 3.

NEW COVENANT REFERENCES

I and My Father are One. - *Yochanan (John) 10:30 KJV*

For there are three that bear record in Heaven, the Father, the Word, and the Holy Spirit: and these three are One. – *I John 5:7 KJV*

GOD and the Nature of Light, a Copy and Shadow

Light is broken down into three primary colors: Blue, Red, and Yellow.

Out of these three primary colors, we get the Spectrum of Light, which contain the 7 colors of the Rainbow: Yellow, Orange, Red, Green, Blue, Indigo, and Violet.

The following Scripture reveals the Sevenfold qualities of God's Holy Spirit:

And the 1 Spirit of the LORD shall rest upon Him--the 2 Spirit of wisdom and 3 Understanding, the 4 Spirit of counsel and 5 Might, the 6 Spirit of knowledge and of the reverential and obedient 7 fear of the LORD. - *Isaiah 11:2*

NEW COVENANT REFERENCES

And this is the message [the message of promise] which we have heard from Him and now are reporting to you: God is Light, and there is no darkness in Him at all [no, not in any way]. - *I Yochanan (John) 1:5*

Immediately I was in the Spirit; and behold, a throne set in heaven, and One sat on the throne. And He who sat there was like a jasper and a sardius stone in appearance; and there was a rainbow around the throne, in appearance like an emerald. - *Revelation 4:2-3*

The quality of jasper is crystalline brightness and the quality of the sardius stone is fiery brilliance. The rainbow is the symbol of the covenant God made with Noah to never flood the earth again as it was flooded in Noah's day. God was revealing Himself in the spectrum of light as Yochanan (John) saw this around His throne as recorded in the book of Revelation. (endnote 2)

GENESIS: The First Prophecy

And I will put enmity between you (the serpent) and the woman, and between your offspring and her Offspring; He will bruise and tread your head underfoot, and you will lie in wait and bruise His heel. - *Genesis 3:15*

NEW COVENANT REFERENCES

Then he delivered Him over to them to be crucified. And they took Jesus and led [Him] away; so He went out, bearing His own cross, to the spot called The Place of the Skull--in Hebrew it is called Golgotha.
- *Yochanan (John) 19:16-17*

This Place of the Skull where Yeshua (Jesus) was crucified and made atonement for our sins is symbolic of His "crushing the head of the serpent", that is, the devil.

But when the fullness of the time was come, God sent forth His Son, made of a woman, made under the law, To redeem them that were under the law, that we might receive the adoption as sons. - *Galatians 4:4*

Yeshua's (Jesus') death on the cross as the perfect, spotless Lamb of God Who takes away the sins of the world ensured satan's ultimate defeat: the treading of his head (symbol of power and authority) underfoot.

Blotting out the handwriting of ordinances that was against us, which was contrary to us, and took it out of the way, nailing it to His cross; and having spoiled principalities and powers, He made a show of them openly, triumphing over them in it. - *Colossians 2:14-15*

The devil thought he was thwarting the plan of God by crucifying the Messiah, Yeshua (Jesus):

But we speak the wisdom of God in a mystery, even the hidden wisdom, which God ordained before the world unto our glory: which none of the princes of this world knew: for had they known it, they would not have crucified the Lord of glory. - *I Corinthians 2:7-8 KJV*

TANAKH REFERENCES

He leads princes away spoiled, and overthrows the mighty. - *Job 12:19 KJV*

He shall cut off the spirit of princes; He is awesome to the kings of the earth. - *Psalm 76:12a NKJV*

He was bruised for our guilt and iniquities. - *Isaiah 53:5*

GENESIS: He Took the Curse for Us

Thorns also and thistles shall it bring forth for you, and you shall eat the plants of the field. - *Genesis 3:18*

Because of the first man Adam's sin, the ground of the earth was cursed with thorns. Yeshua (Jesus) took the curse of mankind upon Himself, symbolized by the crown of thorns. He took the curse so we could be blessed. This is the unfailing, everlasting Love of God for us.

NEW COVENANT REFERENCES

Then the governor's soldiers took Jesus into the palace, and they gathered the whole battalion about Him.

And they stripped off His clothes and put a scarlet robe (garment of dignity and office worn by Roman officers of rank) upon Him.

And, weaving a crown of thorns, they put it on His head and put a reed (staff) in His right hand. And kneeling before Him, they made sport of Him, saying, Hail (greetings, good health to You, long life to You), King of the Jews! - *Matthew 27:27-29*

Christ purchased our freedom [redeeming us] from the curse (doom) of the Law [and its condemnation] by [Himself] becoming a curse for us, for it is written [in the Scriptures], Cursed is everyone who hangs on a tree (is crucified); [Deut. 21:23] - *Galatians 3:13*

The tree in this verse speaks of the cross of wood on which Jesus gave His life for us.

GENESIS: the Pre-Flood Patriarchs

The Gospel was Hidden in the Meaning of their Names (endnote 3):

ADAM - Man (specifically, Mankind)

SETH - To place or appoint

ENOSH - Mortal (frailty or misery)

KENAN - Immovable (negatively as in mourning or dirge)

MAHALALEL - Blessed (Praise of God)

JARED - To descend (or "will come down")

ENOCH - Initiating (or to train or teach)

METHUSELAH - His death will release

LAMECH - Grieving

NOAH - Rest

When you put the meanings together, it reads like this:

Mankind is appointed mortal frailty and misery. The Blessed Praise of God will descend (come down), teaching. His death will release grieving to rest.

GENESIS: Melchizedek, the Pre-Incarnate Messiah

Then Melchizedek king of Salem brought out bread and wine; he was the priest of God Most High. And he blessed him (Abram) and said:

"Blessed be Abram of God Most High, Possessor of heaven and earth; And blessed be God Most High, Who has delivered your enemies into your hand." And he gave him a tithe of all. - *Genesis 14:18-20 NKJV*

Salem (from "Shalom") means "peace". King of Salem, King (or Prince) of peace.

NEW COVENANT REFERENCES

*This hope we have as an Anchor of the soul, both sure and steadfast, and which enters the Presence behind the veil,

Where the forerunner has entered for us, even Jesus, having become High Priest forever according to the order of Melchizedek. - *Hebrews 6:19- 20 NKJV*

For this Melchizedek, king of Salem, priest of the Most High God, Who met Abraham returning from the slaughter of the kings and blessed him.

To whom also Abraham gave a tenth part of all, first being translated "King of righteousness", and then also king of Salem, meaning "King of peace",

Without father, without mother, without genealogy, have neither beginning of days nor end of life, but made like the Son of God, remains a priest continually. - *Hebrews 7:1-3 NKJV*

TANAKH REFERENCE

For unto us a Child is born, unto us a Son is given: and the government shall be upon His shoulder: and His name shall be called Wonderful, Counselor, The Mighty God, The Everlasting Father, The Prince of Peace. - *Isaiah 9:6- 7 KJV*

GENESIS: The Angel of the Lord, Pre-Incarnate Appearances of our Messiah, Yeshua (Jesus Christ)

5 Then Sarai said to Abram, May [the responsibility for] my wrong and deprivation of rights be upon you! I gave my maid into your bosom, and when she saw that she was with child, I was contemptible and despised in her eyes. May the Lord be the judge between you and me. 6 But Abram said to Sarai, See here, your maid is in your hands and power; do as you please with her. And when Sarai dealt severely with her, humbling and afflicting her, she [Hagar] fled from her. 7 But the Angel of the Lord found her by a spring of water in the wilderness on the road to Shur. 8 And He said, Hagar, Sarai's maid, where did you come from, and where are you intending to go? And she said, I am running away from my mistress Sarai. 9 The Angel of the Lord said to her, Go back to your mistress and [humbly] submit to her control. 10 Also the Angel of the Lord said to her, I will multiply your descendants exceedingly, so that they shall not be numbered for multitude. 11 And the Angel of the Lord continued, See now, you are with child and shall bear a son, and shall call his name Ishmael [God hears], because the Lord has heard and paid attention to your affliction. 12 And he [Ishmael] will be as a wild ass among men; his

hand will be against every man and every man's hand against him, and he will live to the east and on the borders of all his kinsmen. 13 So she called the name of the Lord Who spoke to her, You are a God of seeing, for she said, Have I [not] even here [in the wilderness] looked upon Him Who sees me [and lived]?.. - *Genesis 16:5-13*

In verse 13 of this discourse, she addresses God the Almighty (El). His title as the Angel of the Lord in this chapter begins in verse 7. The Hebrew word for "Angel" in this context is "*malak" meaning to dispatch as a deputy; a messenger, spec. of God, i.e. an angel (also a prophet, priest or teacher): - ambassador, angel, king, messenger. Messiah Yeshua is all of these and much more. (endnote 4)

These appearances are found sporadically from Genesis to Malachi. Abraham, Moses and Gideon as well as Samson's parents experienced these visitations from Him. Also, with Daniel and his two friends in the fiery furnace as "the form of the fourth is like the Son of God" (Daniel 3:25).

NEW COVENANT REFERENCE

For to which of the angels did [God] ever say, You are My Son, today I have begotten You [established You in an official Sonship relation, with kingly dignity]? And again, I will be to Him a Father, and He will be to Me a Son? - *Hebrews 1:5*

10 GENESIS: God Will Provide a Lamb, a Foreshadow

[God] said, Take now your son, your only son Isaac, whom you love, and go to the region of Moriah; and offer him there as a burnt offering upon one of the mountains of which I will tell you...

On the third day Abraham looked up and saw the place in the distance...

Abraham said, My son, God Himself will provide a lamb...

And Abraham stretched forth his hand and took hold of the knife to slay his son.

But the Angel of the Lord called to him from heaven...and He said, Do not lay your hand on the lad or do anything to him; for now I know that you fear and revere God, since you have not held back from Me or begrudged giving Me your son, your only son.

Then Abraham looked up and glanced around, and behold, behind him was a ram* caught in a thicket by his horns. And Abraham went and took the ram and offered it up for a burnt offering and an ascending sacrifice instead of his son!

So Abraham called the name of that place The Lord Will Provide. And it is said to this day, On the mount of the Lord it will be provided. - *Genesis 22:2, 4, 8, 10-11, 13-14*

*A ram is a male lamb, being symbolic of Jesus the Messiah. Thus the theme of substitutionary atonement for sin is laced throughout the Mosaic Scriptures as a prophetic foreshadowing.

NEW COVENANT REFERENCES

The next day John saw Jesus coming to him and said, Look! There is the Lamb of God, Who takes away the sin of the world! - *Yochanan (John) 1:29*

For God so loved the world, that He gave His only begotten Son, that whosoever believes in Him should not perish, but have Everlasting Life. - *Yochanan (John) 3:16 KJV*

By faith Abraham, when he was put to the test [while the testing of his faith was still in progress], had already brought Isaac for an offering; he who had gladly received and welcomed [God's] promises was ready to sacrifice his only son. - *Hebrews 11:17*

11
GENESIS: Messiah, Abraham's Seed

In blessing I will bless you and in multiplying I will multiply your descendants like the stars of the heavens and like the sand on the seashore. And your Seed (Heir) will possess the gate of His enemies.

And in your Seed [Christ] shall all the nations of the earth be blessed and [by Him] bless themselves, because you have heard and obeyed My voice. - *Genesis 22:17-18*

NEW COVENANT REFERENCES

For when God made [His] promise to Abraham, He swore by Himself, since He had no one greater by whom to swear, saying, Blessing I certainly will bless you and multiplying I will multiply you. - *Hebrews 6:13-14*

So from one man, though he was physically as good as dead, there have sprung descendants whose number is as the stars of heaven and as countless as the innumerable sands on the seashore. - *Hebrews 11:12*

You are the descendents (sons) of the prophets and the heirs of the covenant which God made and gave to your forefathers, saying to Abraham, And in your Seed (Heir) shall all the families of the earth be blessed and benefited.

It was to you first that God sent His Servant and Son Jesus, when He raised Him up [provided and gave Him for us], to bless you in turning every one of you from your wickedness and evil ways. - *Acts 3:25-26*

Now the promises (covenants, agreements) were decreed and made to Abraham and his Seed (his Offspring, his Heir), He [God] does not say, And to seeds (descendants, heirs), as if referring to many persons, but, And to your Seed (your Descendant, your Heir), obviously referring to one individual, Who is [none other than] Christ (the Messiah).
- *Galatians 3:16*

GENESIS: The Lion of Judah, a Foreshadow

Judah, a lions cub! With the prey, my son, you have gone high up [the mountain]. He stooped down, he crouched like a lion, and like a lioness--who dares provoke and rouse Him?

The scepter or leadership shall not depart from Judah, nor the ruler's staff from between His feet, until Shiloh (the Messiah, the Peaceful One) comes to Whom it belongs, and to Him shall be the obedience of the people. - *Genesis 49:9-10*

NEW COVENANT REFERENCES

For it is evident that our Lord sprang out of Judah; - *Hebrews 7:14a NKJV*

Then one of the elders (of the Heavenly Sanhedrin) said to me, Stop weeping! See, the Lion of the tribe of Judah, the Root (Source) of David, has won (has overcome and conquered)! He can open the scroll and break its seven seals! - *Revelation 5:5*

TANAKH REFERENCES

He speaks, who heard the words of God and knew the knowledge of the Most High, who saw the vision of the Almighty, falling down, but having his eyes open and uncovered:

I see Him, but not now; I behold Him, but He is not near. A Star shall come forth out of Jacob, and a Scepter shall rise out of Israel and shall crush all the corners of Moab and break down all the sons of Sheth (Moab's sons of tumult). - *Numbers 24:16-17*

The lion has roared, who will not fear? The Lord GOD has spoken, who can but prophesy? - *Amos 3:8 KJV*

EXODUS: The Passover Lamb, a Foreshadow

They shall take of the blood and put it on the two side posts and on the lintel [above the door space] of the houses in which they shall eat [the Passover lamb]. - *Exodus 12:7*

The blood of the Passover Lamb sprinkled on the lintel and door posts (of a wooden door) speaks of the cross on which Yeshua (Jesus) gave His life for our Atonement. Yeshua said "I am the door of the sheep" in Yochanan (John) 10:7. When Yeshua (Jesus) laid down His life for us, it was on a Passover.

John the Baptist said by the Holy Spirit "Behold the Lamb of God, Who takes away the sins of the world". His spiritual eyes discerned his Messiah; and even as an unborn babe, he sensed Him when he leaped in his mother Elizabeth's womb upon her greeting her cousin Mary (Yeshua's mother when on earth).

NEW COVENANT REFERENCES

The next day John saw Jesus coming to him and said, Look! There is the Lamb of God, Who takes away the sin of the world! - *Yochanan (John) 1:29*

Now before the Passover Feast began, Jesus knew (was fully aware) that the time had come for Him to leave this world and return to the Father. And as He had loved those who were His own in the world, He loved them to the last and to the highest degree. - *Yochanan (John) 13:1*

How much more surely shall the blood of Christ, Who by virtue of [His] eternal Spirit [His own preexistent divine personality] has offered Himself as an unblemished sacrifice to God, purify our consciences from dead works and lifeless observances to serve the [ever] living God?

[Christ, the Messiah] is therefore the Negotiator and Mediator of an [entirely] new agreement (testament, covenant), so that those who are called and offered it may receive the fulfillment of the promised everlasting inheritance--since a death has taken place which rescues and delivers and redeems them from the transgressions committed under the [old] first agreement. - *Hebrews 9:14-15*

TANAKH REFERENCE

...For it is the blood that makes an atonement for the soul. - *Leviticus 17:11 NKJV*

Jesus laid down His life on a Passover, which was another fulfillment of His role as the Lamb of God.

EXODUS: Hyssop, a Foreshadow of Cleansing

And you shall take a bunch of hyssop, dip it in the blood in the basin, and touch the lintel above the door and the two side posts with the blood; and none of you shall go out of his house until morning. - *Exodus 12:22*

Purge me with hyssop, and I shall be clean: wash me, and I shall be whiter than snow. - *Psalm 51:7 NKJV (spoken by king David during his prayer of repentance from sin)*

NEW COVENANT REFERENCES

After this, Jesus, knowing that all was now finished (ended), said in fulfillment of the Scripture, "I thirst" (Ps 69:21).

A vessel (jar) full of sour wine (vinegar) was placed there, so they put a sponge soaked in the sour wine on [a stalk, reed of] hyssop, and held it to [His] mouth.

When Jesus had received the sour wine, He said, "It is finished!" And He bowed His head and gave up His spirit. - *Yochanan (John) 19:28-30 (words of Yeshua [Jesus] after His crucifixion)*

Hyssop is known as an herb with a cleansing and healing effect on the body. A stalk of Hyssop is seen in Exodus 22 as the means by which the blood of the Passover lamb is applied. It is mentioned in Psalm 51 by King David in his prayer of repentance from sin. A stalk of Hyssop was also used at the place of Yeshua's crucifixion, as written in the B'rit Hadashah (New Testament). Hyssop is linked in the Scriptures with protection, covering, repentance, cleansing and atonement. This is woven into the Scriptures as part of a foreshadow of Messiah's atonement. Nothing is wasted in the Scriptures, as the Almighty God has meaning and purpose for everything contained therein. Hyssop is mentioned twelve times in the Bible.

It is interesting to note that the verse in Exodus pertaining to the application of the Passover lamb's blood is found in verse 22. Psalm 22 is the most prophetic messianic Psalm of the crucifixion of Messiah Yeshua (Christ Jesus), as you will see later in this book. Genesis 22 shows the foreshadow of the substitutionary ram (male lamb) God provided Abraham in place of giving his son. Isaiah 22:22 speaks of the key of David. God's Word is perfect.

EXODUS: The Lamb, Not One Bone Broken

In one house shall it be eaten [by one company]; you shall not carry any of the flesh outside the house; neither shall you break a bone of it. - *Exodus 12:46*

NEW COVENANT REFERENCE

When Jesus had received the sour wine, He said, It is finished! And He bowed His head and gave up His spirit.

Since it was the day of Preparation, in order to prevent the bodies from hanging on the cross on the Sabbath--for that Sabbath was a very solemn and important one--the Jews requested Pilate to have the legs broken and the bodies taken away.

So the soldiers came and broke the legs of the first one, and of the other who had been crucified with Him.

*33 But when they came to Jesus and they saw that He was already dead, they did not break His legs...

And he who saw it (the eyewitness) gives this evidence, and his testimony is true; and he knows that he tells the truth, that you may believe also.

For these things took place, that the Scripture might be fulfilled (verified, carried out), Not one of His bones shall be broken. - *Yochanan (John) 19:30-33, 35-36*

TANAKH REFERENCES

They shall leave none of it until the morning nor break any bone of it; according to all the statues for the Passover they shall keep it. - *Numbers 9:12*

He keeps all His bones; not one of them is broken. - *Psalm 34:20*

Crucifixion brings about death by suffocation. Breaking the legs of the victims would bring it about quicker, as they would have to push up on their feet to catch a breath. Yeshua (Jesus) was already dead before they could do this, so this prophecy would be fulfilled.

*It's interesting to note that Yeshua (Jesus) laid down His life at age 33, and in the New Covenant reference from Yochanan (John), it is in verse 33 that the soldiers found He was dead.

EXODUS: Bitter Waters Made Sweet, a Foreshadow of the Cross

When they came to Marah, they could not drink its waters for they were bitter; therefore it was named Marah [bitterness].

The people murmured against Moses, saying, What shall we drink?

And he cried to the Lord, and the Lord showed him a tree which he cast into the waters, and the waters were made sweet. There [the Lord] made for them a statute and an ordinance, and there He proved them. - *Exodus 15:23-25*

When Yeshua (Jesus) Messiah atoned for our sins on the cross by shedding His divine Blood, it brought Salvation to mankind, for all who come to Him. Healing for souls and also bodies (see Isaiah 53:5).

NEW COVENANT REFERENCE

The God of our forefathers raised up Jesus, Whom you killed by hanging Him on a tree (cross).

God exalted Him to His right hand to be Prince and Leader and Savior and Deliverer and Preserver, in order to grant repentance to Israel and to bestow forgiveness and release from sins. - *Acts 5:30-31*

EXODUS: Manna, Bread from Heaven, a Foreshadow

And when the dew had gone, behold, upon the face of the wilderness there lay a fine, round and flake-like thing, as fine as hoarfrost on the ground.

When the Israelites saw it, they said one to another, Manna [what is it?]. For they did not know what it was. And Moses said to them, This is the bread which the Lord has given you to eat. - *Exodus 16:14-15*

NEW COVENANT REFERENCE

Our forefathers ate the manna in the wilderness; as the Scripture says, He gave them bread out of heaven to eat.

Jesus then said to them, I assure you, most solemnly I tell you, Moses did not give you the Bread from heaven [what Moses gave you was not the Bread from heaven], but it is My Father Who gives you the true heavenly Bread.

For the Bread of God is He Who comes down out of heaven and gives Life to the world.

Then they said to Him, Lord, give us this bread always (all the time)!

Jesus replied, I Am the Bread of Life. He who comes to Me will never be hungry, and he who believes in and cleaves to and trusts in and relies on Me will never thirst any more (at any time). - *Yochanan (John) 6:31-35*

TANAKH REFERENCES

You gave them bread from heaven for their hunger and brought water for them out of the rock for their thirst; and You told them to go in and possess the land You had sworn to give them. - *Nehemiah 9:15*

Yet He commanded the clouds above and opened the doors of heaven; And He rained down upon them manna to eat and gave them heaven's grain. - *Psalm 78:23-24*

EXODUS: Blood of the Covenant, a Foreshadow

And Moses took half of the blood and put it in basins, and half of the blood he dashed against the altar.

Then he took the Book of the Covenant and read in the hearing of the people; and they said, All that the Lord has said we will do, and we will be obedient.

And Moses took the [remaining half of the] blood and sprinkled it on the people, and said, Behold the blood of the covenant which the Lord has made with you in accordance with all these words. - *Exodus 24:6-8*

NEW COVENANT REFERENCES

And He took the cup, and when He had given thanks, He gave it to them, saying, Drink of it, all of you; For this is My blood of the new covenant, which [ratifies the agreement and] is being poured out for many for the forgiveness of sins. - *Matthew 26:27-28*

And He said to them, This is My blood [which ratifies] the new covenant, [the blood] which is being poured out for (on account of) many. - *Mark 14:24*

And in like manner, He took the cup after supper, saying, This cup is the new testament or covenant [ratified] in My blood, which is shed (poured out) for you. - *Luke 22:20*

In Leviticus 17:11, the Scripture says it is the blood that makes atonement for the soul. Throughout the Tanakh, the blood has been a theme: a foreshadow of the Messiah Yeshua's (Jesus') sacrifice.

TANAKH REFERENCE

What shall I render to the LORD for all His benefits toward me? I will take the cup of Salvation, and call upon the Name of the LORD. - *Psalm 116:12-13*

In the old custom of Jewish engagement, the man offered a cup to the woman he wanted to marry. If she took the cup and drank from it, that meant she accepted his offer. This cup of salvation was prophesied of in Psalm 116 and fulfilled by Yeshua (Jesus) Messiah in Matthew 26. God offers His Salvation to us through His Son Yeshua (Jesus). When we say "Yes", we are taking His cup of salvation; we are calling upon the Name of the Lord. Jesus is Lord!

EXODUS: The Mercy Seat, a Foreshadow

And the LORD said to Moses,...

And you shall make a mercy seat (a covering) of pure gold, two cubits and a half long and a cubit and a half wide.

And you shall make two cherubim (winged angelic figures) of [solid] hammered gold on the two ends of the mercy seat.

Make one cherub on each end, making the cherubim of one piece with the mercy seat, on the two ends of it.

And the cherubim shall spread out their wings above, covering the mercy seat with their wings, facing each other and looking down toward the mercy seat. - *Exodus 25:1, 17-20*

NEW COVENANT REFERENCES

For as yet they did not know (understand) the statement of Scripture that He must rise again from the dead. [Ps. 16:10].

Then the disciples went back again to their homes (lodging places).

But Mary remained standing outside the tomb sobbing. As she wept, she stooped down [and looked] into the tomb.

And she saw two angels in white sitting there, one at the head and one at the feet, where the body of Jesus had lain. - *Yochanan (John) 20:9-12*

[All] are justified and made upright and in right standing with God, freely and gratuitously by His grace (His unmerited favor and mercy), through the redemption which is [provided] in Christ Jesus,

Whom God put forward [before the eyes of all] as a mercy seat and propitiation by His blood [the cleansing and life-giving sacrifice of atonement and reconciliation, to be received] through faith. - *Romans 3:24-25a*

Exodus 25 shows a prophetic picture of God's true mercy seat. Yeshua (Jesus) gave His life for us, leading to the tomb and concluding His atonement path with His Resurrection from the dead. The word "propitiation" in the Greek text is "hilasterion", which means, "mercy seat".

EXODUS: The Ark and the Bread, a Foreshadow

And Moses said to Aaron, Take a pot and put an omer of manna in it, and lay it up before the Lord, to be kept throughout your generations. As the Lord commanded Moses, Aaron laid it up before the Testimony to be kept [in the ark]. - *Exodus 16:33-34*

And you shall set the showbread (the bread of the Presence) on the table before Me always. - *Exodus 25:30*

NEW COVENANT REFERENCES

Just as the living Father sent Me and I live by (through, because of) the Father, even so whoever continues to feed on Me [whoever takes Me for his food and is nourished by Me] shall [in his turn] live through and because of Me.

This is the Bread that came down from Heaven. It is not like the manna which our forefathers ate, and yet died; he who takes this Bread for his food shall live forever. - *Yochanan (John) 6:57-58*

But [inside] beyond the second curtain or veil, [there stood another] tabernacle [division] known as the Holy of Holies.

It had the golden altar of incense and the ark (chest) of the covenant, covered over with wrought gold. This [ark] contained a golden jar which held the manna and the rod of Aaron that sprouted and the [two stone] slabs of the covenant [bearing the Ten Commandments]. - *Hebrews 9:3-4*

Prophetic interpretation: The Mercy seat (His tomb), the manna (Messiah the Living Bread from Heaven), and Aaron's Rod sprouted (Resurrection).

EXODUS: Strike the Rock, Water Shall Come Out

Behold, I will stand before you there on the rock at [Mount] Horeb; and you shall strike the rock, and water shall come out of it, that the people may drink, And Moses did so in the sight of the elders of Israel. - Exodus 17:6

NEW COVENANT REFERENCES

But one of the soldiers pierced His side with a spear, and immediately Blood and water came (flowed) out. - *Yochanan (John) 19:34*

And they all drank the same spiritual (supernaturally given) drink. For they drank from a spiritual Rock which followed them [produced by the sole power of God Himself without natural instrumentality], and the Rock was Christ. - *I Corinthians 10:4*

The Rock is Christ Jesus; Messiah Yeshua. The water is spiritual drink and these are foreshadowed by the Rock and the Water in Exodus 17:6. The reference of His side being pierced, with blood and water flowing out is also foreshadowed by Exodus 17:6 by Moses striking the Rock, as the Lord had instructed him.

EXODUS: The Veil of the Temple

You shall erect the tabernacle after the plan of it shown you on the mountain.

And make a veil of blue, purple, and scarlet [stuff] and fine twined linen, skillfully worked with cherubim on it...

*33. And you shall hang the veil from the clasps and bring the ark of the Testimony into place within the veil; and the veil shall separate for you the Holy Place from the Most Holy Place... - *Exodus 26:30-31, 33*

Yeshua (Jesus) Messiah, being the mediator between God and man, destroyed the barrier that was between God and man by His own Blood, enabling mankind (who come to Him) to enter the Holy of Holies (God's Presence). The tearing of the Veil (curtain) was symbolic of this. He gave His life for us at age thirty three (33).* See Exodus 26:33 above speaking of the veil.

It has been verified in the writings of the Talmud that the veil of the temple was torn in two.

NEW COVENANT REFERENCES

And Jesus cried again with a loud voice and gave up His spirit. And at once the curtain of the sanctuary of the temple was torn in two from top to bottom; the earth shook and the rocks were split. - *Matthew 27:50-51*

While the sun's light faded or was darkened; and the curtain [of the Holy of Holies] of the temple was torn in two. - *Luke 23:45*

Therefore, brethren, since we have full freedom and confidence to enter into the [Holy of] Holies [by the power and virtue] in the Blood of Jesus, By this fresh (new) and living way which He initiated and dedicated and opened for us through the separating curtain (veil of the Holy of Holies), that is, through His flesh, - *Hebrews 10:19-20*

By giving His life as an atonement for our sin, He made the way for us to enter in.

EXODUS: The Door, a Foreshadow

You shall make a hanging [to form a screen] for the door of the tent of blue, purple, and scarlet [stuff] and fine twined linen, embroidered.
- *Exodus 26:36*

Everything in the Holy Scriptures has meaning, as God Himself wrote them through holy men of God by His Spirit.

NEW COVENANT REFERENCE

I am the Door; anyone who enters in through Me will be saved (will live). He will come in and he will go out [freely], and will find pasture.
- *Yochanan (John) 10:9*

EXODUS: Urim and Thummim, Lights and Perfection

In the breastplate of judgment you shall put the Urim and the Thummim [unspecified articles used when the high priest asked God's counsel for all Israel]; they shall be upon Aaron's heart when he goes in before the Lord, and Aaron shall bear the judgment (rights, judicial decisions) of the Israelites upon his heart before the Lord continually. - *Exodus 28:30*

These articles were used by the high priest to discern the voice and the will of Almighty God. There is a New Covenant answer to this Scripture. It contains the meaning of the words Urim and Thummim - lights and perfection.

NEW COVENANT REFERENCE

Every good gift and every perfect gift is from above, and comes down from the Father of lights, with whom there is no variation or shadow of turning.

Of His own will He brought us forth by the word of truth, that we might be a kind of firstfruits of His creation. - *James 1:17-18 NKJV*

Today we no longer need the Urim and Thummim nor a human priest to discern the voice of God. Our High Priest is Yeshua (Jesus) Messiah, and He baptizes us with His Holy Spirit (and fire). Through the Holy Spirit of God we receive His leading, guidance, counsel, and hear God's Voice in our hearts. The fire of God's Spirit purifies us. The Holy Spirit is God's perfect gift to us because He is the Spirit of Jesus our Lord. It is through God's precious Holy Spirit that we are born again by the Word of Truth; the Gospel of our Salvation. Then we become light in the Lord. Jesus said we are the light of the world. It is the light of God that shines through us and in us when we receive Jesus and are spiritually reborn.

The Urim and Thummim were upon Aaron's heart when he discerned the voice of God through them. Today, God fills us with His Holy Spirit in our hearts to hear His still small Voice within.

EXODUS: Pomegranates, a Foreshadow

Make the robe [to be worn beneath] the ephod all of blue...And you shall make pomegranates of blue, purple, and scarlet [stuff] around about its skirts, with gold bells between them; - *Exodus 28:31, 33*

The average pomegranate contains approximately 613 seeds. There are 613 laws in the Torah. When you cut a pomegranate in half from top to bottom, there are four sections of seeds, with the dividing walls inside the fruit being in the shape of a + (cross). The pomegranate is blood red, and the seeds look like red droplets.

NEW COVENANT REFERENCES

Do not think that I have come to do away with or undo the Law or the Prophets; I have come not to do away with or undo but to complete and fulfill them. - *Matthew 5:17*

No one has greater Love [no one has shown stronger affection] than to lay down (give up) his own life for his friends. - *John 15:13*

Love does no wrong to one's neighbor [it never hurts anybody]. Therefore Love meets all the requirements and is the fulfilling of the Law. - *Romans 13:10*

When Yeshua (Jesus) Messiah gave His Life for us on the cross, shedding His Blood, He fulfilled the Law, as the Scripture says.

If you take 613 and divide it by 4 (sections of the pomegranate), you get 153.25. One of the most prophetic messianic Scriptures on the Atonement is found in Isaiah 53.

EXODUS: The Lampstand, a Prophetic Symbol

And he made of pure gold its seven lamps, its snuffers, and its ashtrays. Of a talent of pure gold he made the Lampstand and all its utensils. He also made the holy anointing oil [symbol of the Holy Spirit] and the pure, fragrant incense, after the perfumer's art. - *Exodus 37:23-24, 29*

NEW COVENANT REFERENCES

In Him was Life, and the Life was the Light of men. And the Light shines on in the darkness, for the darkness has never overpowered it...

There it was--the true Light [was then] coming into the world [the genuine, perfect, steadfast Light] that illumines every person. - *Yochanan (John) 1:4-5, 9*

Yochanan (John) to the seven assemblies (churches) that are in Asia: May grace (God's unmerited favor) be granted to you and spiritual peace (the peace of Christ's kingdom) from Him Who is and Who was and Who is to come, and from the seven Spirits [the sevenfold Holy Spirit] before His throne,

And from Jesus Christ the faithful and trustworthy Witness, the First-born of the dead [first to be brought back to life] and the Prince (Ruler) of the kings of the earth. To Him Who ever loves us and has once [for all] loosed and freed us from our sins by His own Blood. - *Revelation 1:4-5*

TANAKH REFERENCES

And there shall come forth a Shoot out of the stock of Jesse [David's father], and a Branch out of his roots shall grow and bear fruit. And the Spirit of the Lord shall rest upon Him--the Spirit of wisdom and under-standing, the Spirit of counsel and might, the Spirit of knowledge and of the reverential and obedient fear of the Lord. - *Isaiah 11:1-2*

For behold, upon the stone which I have set before Joshua, upon that one stone are seven eyes or facets [the all-embracing providence of God and the seven-fold radiations of the Spirit of God]. Behold I will carve upon it its inscription, says the Lord of hosts, and I will remove the iniquity and guilt of this land in a single day. - *Zechariah 3:9*

...And said to me, What do you see? I said, I see, and behold, a Lamp-stand of all gold, with its bowl [for oil] on top of it and its seven lamps on it, and [there are] seven pipes to each of the seven lamps which are upon the top of it. - *Zechariah 4:2*

EXODUS: He Suffered Outside the Camp (City)

But the flesh of the bull, its hide, and the contents of its entrails you shall burn with fire outside the camp; it is a sin offering. - *Exodus 29:14*

NEW COVENANT REFERENCE

Therefore Jesus also suffered and died outside the [city's] gate in order that He might purify and consecrate the people through [the shedding of] His own Blood and set them apart as holy [for God]. - *Hebrews 13:12*

EXODUS: The Bread of His Presence, a Foreshadow

He set the bread [of the Presence] in order on it before the Lord, as the Lord had commanded him. - *Exodus 40:23*

NEW COVENANT REFERENCE

For the Bread of God is He Who comes down out of heaven and gives life to the world.

Then they said to Him, Lord, give us this bread always (all the time)!

Jesus replied, I am the Bread of Life. He who comes to Me will never be hungry, and he who believes in and cleaves to and trusts in and relies on Me will never thirst any more (at any time). - *Yochanan (John) 6:32-35*

LEVITICUS & NUMBERS: The Blood Sprinkled Seven Times (7 References) - 6 Foreshadows, the 7th, a Fulfillment

Under the First Covenant, the priests (Levites) were instructed to sprinkle the blood of animals sacrificed for sins seven times:

1. And the priest shall dip his finger in the blood, and sprinkle of the blood seven times before the LORD, before the veil of the sanctuary. - *Leviticus 4:6*

2. And the priest shall dip his finger in some of the blood, and sprinkle it seven times before the LORD, even before the veil. - *Leviticus 4:17*

3. And he shall take the cedar wood, and the hyssop, and the scarlet, and the living bird, and dip them in the blood of the slain bird, and in the running water, and sprinkle the house seven times: - *Leviticus 14:51*

4. And he shall take of the blood of the bullock, and sprinkle it with his finger upon the mercy seat eastward; and before the mercy seat shall he sprinkle of the blood with his finger seven times. - *Leviticus 16:14*

5. And he shall sprinkle of the blood upon it with his finger seven times, and cleanse it, and hallow it from the uncleanness of the children of Israel. - *Leviticus 16:19*

6. And Eleazar the priest shall take of her blood with his finger, and sprinkle of her blood directly before the tabernacle of the congregation seven times. - *Numbers 19:4*

During His crucifixion, Yeshua (Jesus) was wounded in seven places: 1. His head, 2. His back, 3 & 4. His two hands, 5 & 6. His two feet, 7. His side. The cedar wood, hyssop and scarlet in Leviticus 14:51 represents the cross, cleansing, and the Blood of Yeshua (Jesus).

NEW COVENANT REFERENCE

7. Neither by the blood of goats and calves, but by His own Blood He entered in once into the holy place, having obtained eternal redemption for us.

For if the blood of bulls and of goats, and the ashes of an heifer sprinkling the unclean, sanctifies to the purifying of the flesh:

How much more shall the blood of Christ, Who through the eternal Spirit offered Himself without spot to God, purge your conscience from dead works to serve the living God? - *Hebrews 9:12-14 KJV*

NUMBERS: The Serpent on a Pole, a Foreshadow

And the LORD said to Moses, Make a fiery serpent [of bronze] and set it on a pole; and everyone who is bitten, when he looks at it, shall live.

And Moses made a serpent of bronze and put it on a pole, and if a serpent had bitten any man, when he looked to the serpent of bronze [attentively, expectantly, with a steady and absorbing gaze], he lived. - *Numbers 21:8-9*

NEW COVENANT REFERENCES

And just as Moses lifted up the serpent in the desert [on a pole], so must [so it is necessary that] the Son of Man be lifted up [on the cross], in order that everyone who believes in Him [who cleaves to Him, trusts Him, and relies on Him] may not perish, but have eternal life and [actually] live forever! - *Yochanan (John) 3:14-15*

For He has made Him to be sin for us, Who knew no sin; that we might be made the righteousness of God in Him. - *2 Corinthians 5:21*

Yeshua (Jesus) took upon Himself the sins of the whole world. The sins are represented by the serpent. Even today, the medical world uses the symbol of a snake on a pole (T).

NUMBERS: The Star of Bethlehem

I see Him, but not now; I behold Him, but He is not near. A star *(Star) shall come forth out of Jacob, and a scepter (Scepter) shall rise out of Israel and shall crush all the corners of Moab and break down all the sons of Sheth [Moab's sons of tumult]. - *Numbers 24:17*

*This imagery in the hieroglyphic language of the East denotes some eminent ruler. King David as a foreshadow; primarily of the Messiah.

NEW COVENANT REFERENCE

Now when Yeshua (Jesus) was born in Bethlehem of Judea in the days of Herod the king, behold, wise men [astrologers] from the east came to Jerusalem, asking, "Where is He Who has been born King of the Jews? For we have seen His star in the east at its rising and have come to worship Him." - *Matthew 2:1-2*

NUMBERS: Atonement, a Foreshadow at Age 33

...And no atonement can be made for the land, for the blood that is shed on it, except by the blood of him who shed it. - *Numbers 35:33 NKJV*

Under the Old Covenant, the one who took a life had to atone for it. Yeshua (Jesus) shed His own blood to atone for our sins at the age of 33. The Innocent for the guilty. The following 12 New Covenant reference Scriptures about Yeshua laying down His life are also found in verse 33:

NEW COVENANT REFERENCES

And when they came to a place called Golgotha [Latin: Calvary], which means The Place of a Skull ... - *Matthew 27:33 (this is where He was crucified)*

Behold, we are going up to Jerusalem, and the Son of Man will be turned over to the chief priests and the scribes; and they will condemn and sentence Him to death and turn Him over to the Gentiles. - *Mark 10:33*

And He took with Him Peter and James and John, and began to be struck with terror and amazement and deeply troubled and depressed. - *Mark 14:33 (in the Garden Gethsemane before His arrest & crucifixion)*

And when the sixth hour (about midday) had come, there was darkness over the whole land until the ninth hour (about three o'clock). - *Mark 15:33 (on the cross just before He died)*

Nevertheless, I must continue on My way today and tomorrow and the day after that--- for it will never do for a prophet to be destroyed away from Jerusalem! - *Luke 13:33 (Jesus prophesying of His death)*

They will flog Him and kill Him; and on the third day He will rise again. - *Luke 18:33*

And [Simon Peter] said to Him, Lord, I am ready to go with You both to prison and to death. - *Luke 22:33*

And when they came to the place which is called The Skull [Latin: Calvary; Hebrew: Golgotha], there they crucified Him, and [along with] the criminals, one on the right and one on the left. - *Luke 23:33*

Therefore Jesus said, For a little while I am [still] with you, and then I go back to Him Who sent Me. - *Yochanan (John) 7:33*

...He said this to signify in what manner He would die. - *Yochanan (John) 12:33*

[Dear] little children, I am to be with you only a little longer. You will look for Me and, as I told the Jews, so I tell you now: you are not able to come where I am going. - *Yochanan (John) 13:33*

But when they came to Jesus and they saw that He was already dead, they did not break His legs. - *Yochanan (John) 19:33*

DEUTERONOMY: Yeshua, Israel's Salvation and Prophet

But Joshua son of Nun, who stands before you, he shall enter there. Encourage him, for he shall cause Israel to inherit it. - *Deuteronomy 1:38*

This verse speaks of Israel's inheritance of the promised land. Joshua's name in Hebrew is "Yehowshua" meaning "Yahweh-saved". This is the same name translated in the New Testament as "Jesus" (Yeshua).

Joshua is a foreshadow of Jesus Messiah, as he led Israel to the inherited promised land of Canaan. Yeshua (Jesus) the Messiah leads us spiritually into the promise of Salvation.

The LORD your God will raise up for you a prophet (Prophet) from the midst of your brethren like me [Moses]; to him you shall listen.

I will raise up for them a prophet (Prophet) from among their brethren like you, and will put My words in his mouth; and he shall speak to them all that I command him. - *Deuteronomy 18:15, 18*

NEW COVENANT REFERENCES

And when He entered Jerusalem, all the city became agitated and [trembling with excitement] said, Who is This? And the crowds replied, This is the prophet Jesus from Nazareth of Galilee. - *Matthew 21:10-11*

When the people saw the sign (miracle) that Jesus had performed, they began saying, Surely and beyond a doubt this is the Prophet Who is to come into the world! - *Yochanan (John) 6:14*

Thus Moses said to the forefathers, The Lord God will raise up for you a Prophet from among your brethren as [He raised up] me; Him you shall listen to and understand by hearing and heed in all things whatever He tells you. - *Acts 3:22*

DEUTERONOMY: He Spoke on the Father's Authority

I will raise up for them a prophet (Prophet) from among their brethren like you, and will put My words in His mouth; and He shall speak to them all that I command Him. - *Deuteronomy 18:18*

NEW COVENANT REFERENCE

This is because I have never spoken on My own authority or of My own accord or as self-appointed, but the Father Who sent Me has Himself given Me orders [concerning] what to say and what to tell. And I know that His commandment is (means) eternal life. So whatever I speak, I am saying [exactly] what My Father has told Me to say and in accordance with His instructions. - *Yochanan (John) 12:49-50*

DEUTERONOMY: Two or Three Witnesses

...Only on the testimony of two or three witnesses shall a charge be established. - *Deuteronomy 19:15b*

NEW COVENANT REFERENCES

In your [own] Law it is written that the testimony (evidence) of two persons is reliable and valid. I am One [of the Two] bearing testimony concerning Myself; and My Father, Who sent Me, He also testifies about Me. - *Yochanan (John) 8:17-18*

But if he does not listen, take along with you one or two others, so that every word may be confirmed and upheld by the testimony of two or three witnesses. - *Matthew 18:16*

This is the third time I am coming to you. In the mouth of two or three witnesses shall every word be established. - *2 Corinthians 13:1*

In the B'rit Hadashah (New Covenant) Scriptures, the Holy Spirit, Who wrote through the holy men of God, put in the testimonies of four disciples - Matthew, Mark, Luke and Yochanan (John). They testified of Yeshua (Jesus) our Messiah. Of His birth, life, miraculous works, the atoning sacrifice of His life on the cross and His resurrection. This is two witnesses times two!

DEUTERONOMY: A Foreshadow of Taking the Curse

And if a man has committed a sin worthy of death and he is put to death and [afterward] you hang him on a tree, His body shall not remain all night upon the tree, but you shall surely bury him on the same day, for a hanged man is accursed by God. Thus you shall not defile your land which the Lord your God gives you for an inheritance. - *Deuteronomy 21:22-23*

Yeshua (Jesus) hung on the cross (tree) and took the curse of sin and death upon Himself.

NEW COVENANT REFERENCE

Christ purchased our freedom [redeeming us] from the curse (doom) of the Law [and its condemnation] by [Himself] becoming a curse for us, for it is written [in the Scriptures], Cursed is everyone who hangs on a tree (is crucified). - *Galatians 3:13*

JOB: Job's Prophecy

For I know that my Redeemer and Vindicator lives, and at last He [the Last One] will stand upon the earth. - *Job 19:25*

NEW COVENANT REFERENCES

When I saw Him, I fell at His feet as if dead. But He laid His right hand on me and said, Do not be afraid! I am the First and the Last...
- *Revelation 1:17*

And to the angel (messenger) of the assembly (church) in Smyrna write: These are the words of the First and the Last, Who died and came to life again: - *Revelation 2:8*

I am the Alpha and the Omega, the First and the Last (the Before all and the End of all). - *Revelation 22:13*

TANAKH REFERENCES

Thus says the Lord, the King of Israel and His Redeemer, the Lord of hosts: I am the First and I am the Last; besides Me there is no God.
- *Isaiah 44:6*

This Scripture speaks of God as "the Lord, the King of Israel" and His Redeemer, the Lord of hosts (Jesus Christ the Messiah). It is a Father & Son Scripture.

Listen to Me, O Jacob, and Israel, My called [ones]: I am He; I am the First, I also am the Last. - *Isaiah 48:12*

And His feet shall stand in that day upon the Mount of Olives, which lies before Jerusalem on the east, and the Mount of Olives shall be split in two from the east to the west by a very great valley; and half of the mountain shall remove toward the north and half of it toward the south. - *Zechariah 14:4*

The Psalms

PSALM 2: The Son of God

The kings of the earth take their places; the rulers take counsel together against the LORD and His Anointed One (the Messiah, the Christ). - *Psalm 2:2*

Yet have I anointed (installed and placed) My King [firmly] on My holy hill of Zion. I will declare the decree of the Lord: He said to Me, You are My Son; this day [I declare] I have begotten You. - *Psalm 2:6-7*

Kiss the Son [pay homage to Him in purity], lest He be angry and you perish in the way, for soon shall His wrath be kindled. O blessed (happy, fortunate, and to be envied) are all those who seek refuge and put their trust in Him! - *Psalm 2:12*

NEW COVENANT REFERENCES

And there came a voice out from within heaven, You are My Beloved Son; in You I am well pleased. - *Mark 1:11*

For God so greatly loved and dearly prized the world that He [even] gave up His only begotten (unique) Son, so that whoever believes in (trusts in, clings to, relies on) Him shall not perish (come to destruction, be lost) but have Eternal (everlasting) Life. - *Yochanan (John) 3:16*

Who by the mouth of Your servant David has said ... The kings of the earth stood up, and the rulers were gathered together against the Lord, and against His Christ. For of a truth against Your Holy Child Jesus, whom You have anointed, both Herod, and Pontius Pilate, with the Gentiles, and the people of Israel, were gathered together. - *Acts 4:25-27*

This He has completely fulfilled for us, their children, by raising up JESUS, as it is written in the second psalm, You are My Son; today I have begotten You [caused You to arise, to be born; formally shown You to be the Messiah by the resurrection]. - *Acts 13:33*

For to which of the angels did [God] ever say, You are My Son, today I have begotten You [established You in an official Sonship relation, with kingly dignity]? And again, I will be to Him a Father, and He will be to Me a Son? - *Hebrews 1:5*

So too Christ (the Messiah) did not exalt Himself to be made a high priest, But was appointed and exalted by Him Who said to Him, You are My Son; today I have begotten You. - *Hebrews 5:5*

PSALM 14: Salvation (Yeshua) Comes from Zion

Oh, that the Salvation of Israel would come out of Zion! When the Lord shall restore the fortunes of His people, then Jacob shall rejoice and Israel shall be glad. - *Psalm 14:7*

NEW COVENANT REFERENCE

And so all Israel will be saved, As it is written, The Deliverer will come from Zion, He will banish ungodliness from Jacob. And this will be My covenant (My agreement) with them when I shall take away their sins. - *Romans 11:26-27*

TANAKH REFERENCE

He shall come as a Redeemer to Zion and to those in Jacob (Israel) who turn from transgression, says the Lord. - *Isaiah 59:20*

PSALM 16: He Arose from the Dead

For You will not abandon Me to Sheol (the place of the dead), neither will You suffer Your Holy One to see corruption. - *Psalm 16:10*

NEW COVENANT REFERENCES

For as yet they did not know (understand) the statement of Scripture that He must rise again from the dead. - *Yochanan (John) 20:9*

[But] God raised Him up, liberating Him from the pangs of death, seeing that it was not possible for Him to continue to be controlled or retained by it. For David says in regard to Him, I saw the Lord constantly before me, for He is at my right hand that I may not be shaken or overthrown or cast down [from my secure and happy state]. Therefore my heart rejoiced and my tongue exulted exceedingly; moreover, my flesh also will dwell in hope [will encamp, pitch its tent, and dwell in hope in anticipation of the resurrection]. For You will not abandon my soul, leaving it helpless in Hades (the state of departed spirits), nor let Your Holy One know decay or see destruction [of the body after death]. - *Acts 2:23-27*

He, foreseeing this, spoke [by foreknowledge] of the resurrection of the Christ (the Messiah) that He was not deserted [in death] and left in Hades (the state of departed spirits), nor did His body know decay or see destruction. - *Acts 2:31*

And as to His having raised Him from among the dead, now no more to return to [undergo] putrefaction and dissolution [of the grave], He spoke in this way, I will fulfill and give to you the holy and sure mercy and blessings [that were promised and assured] to David. For this reason He says also in another Psalm, You will not allow Your Holy One to see corruption [to undergo putrefaction and dissolution of the grave]. For David, after he had served God's will and purpose and counsel in his own generation, fell asleep [in death] and was buried among his forefathers, and he did see corruption and undergo putrefaction and dissolution [of the grave]. - *Acts 13:34-36*

For I passed on to you first of all what I also had received, that Christ (the Messiah, the Anointed One) died for our sins in accordance with [what] the Scriptures [foretold], that He was buried, that He arose on the third day as the Scriptures foretold... - *I Corinthians 15:3-4*

PSALM 19: The Bridegroom and the Sun, Copies and Shadows

The Heavens declare the glory of God; and the firmament shows His handiwork.

Day unto day utters speech, and night unto night shows knowledge.

There is no speech nor language, where their voice is not heard.

Their line is gone out through all the earth, and their words to the end of the world.

In them He has set a tabernacle for the sun, Which is as a Bridegroom coming out of His chamber, and rejoices as a strong man to run a race. His going forth is from the end of the heaven, and His circuit to the ends of it: and there is nothing hid from the heat thereof.

The law of the Lord is perfect, converting the soul: the testimony of the LORD is sure, making wise the simple. - *Psalm 19:1-7 KJV*

In Malachi, Yeshua (Jesus) is called the "Sun of righteousness." Remember He is the Word of God, (Psalm 19:7). There was also an eclipse the day He was crucified (Matt 27:45).

But to you that fear My name shall the Sun of righteousness arise with healing in His wings. - *Malachi 4:2a NKJV*

Verses four and five of Psalm 19 speak as a copy and shadow of the Son of God, Yeshua (Jesus), as it says of the Heavens, "they declare His glory" and "In them He (God) has set a tabernacle for the sun," and verse five likens the sun to a Bridegroom coming out of His chamber. Verse 6 speaks of "His going forth is from the end of the heaven, and His circuit to the ends of it."

NEW COVENANT REFERENCES

For as the lightning comes from the East, and flashes to the West, so also will the coming of the Son of man be. - *Matthew 24:27 NKJV*

Then shall the kingdom of Heaven be likened to ten virgins, who took their lamps, and went forth to meet the Bridegroom. - *Matthew 25:1 NKJV*

Yeshua (Jesus) is the Heavenly Bridegroom to us who Believe, and we are His Bride (His beloved).

PSALM 22: The Sufferings of the Messiah

My GOD, My God, why have You forsaken Me? Why are You so far from helping Me, and from the words of My groaning? - *Psalm 22:1*

NEW COVENANT REFERENCE

And about the ninth hour (three o'clock) Jesus cried with a loud voice, Eli, Eli, lama sabachthani? -that is, My God, My God, why have You abandoned Me [leaving Me helpless, forsaken and failing Me in My need]? - *Matthew 27:46*

Yeshua (Jesus) felt forsaken because God the Father could not look upon Him, as He was bearing the sins of the world.

PSALM 22: He was Scorned

...I am the scorn of men, and despised by the people. All who see me laugh at me and mock me; they shoot out the lip, they shake the head, saying, "He trusted and rolled himself on the Lord, that He would deliver him. Let Him deliver him, seeing that He delights in him!" - *Psalm 22:6b-8*

NEW COVENANT REFERENCES

And those who passed by spoke reproachfully and abusively and jeered at Him, wagging their heads. And they said, You Who would tear down the sanctuary of the temple and rebuild it in three days, rescue Yourself from death. If You are the Son of God, come down from the cross. - *Matthew 27:39-40*

In the same way the chief priests, with the scribes and elders, made sport of Him, saying, He rescued others from death; Himself He cannot rescue from death. He is the King of Israel? Let Him come down from the cross now, and we will believe in and acknowledge and cleave to Him.
- *Matthew 27:41-42*

He trusts in God; let God deliver Him now if He cares for Him and will have Him, for He said, I am the Son of God. - *Matthew 27:43*

So also the chief priests, with the scribes, made sport of Him to one another, saying, He rescued others [from death]; Himself He is unable to rescue. Let the Christ (the Messiah), the King of Israel, come down now from the cross, that we may see [it] and trust in and rely on Him and adhere to Him! - *Mark 15:31-32b*

Now the people stood by [calmly and leisurely] watching; but the rulers scoffed and sneered (turned up their noses) at Him, saying, He rescued others [from death]; let Him now rescue Himself, if He is the Christ (the Messiah) of God, His Chosen One! - *Luke 23:35*

TANAKH REFERENCE

I have become also a reproach and a taunt to others; when they see me, they shake their heads. - *Psalm 109:25*

PSALM 22: He was Pierced

I am poured out like water, and all My bones are out of joint: My heart is like wax; it has melted within Me. My strength is dried up like a potsherd; and My tongue clings to My jaws; You have brought me to the dust of death. For dogs have surrounded Me; the assembly of the wicked has enclosed Me: they pierced My hands and My feet. - *Psalm 22:14-16*

When Jesus was crucified, they nailed Him to a wooden pole (cross) and drove nails into His hands and feet to hold him upon it. Those same precious hands that brought life and healing to the sick and dying were pierced. Those feet that walked the streets of Jerusalem and the hills of Galilee and that brought the message of Salvation (for He was and is Salvation) were pierced. They were pierced for you and for me; to make Atonement for our souls. His Love is unfailing.

NEW COVENANT REFERENCE

And again another Scripture says, "They shall look on Him whom they pierced." - *Yochanan (John) 19:37*

TANAKH REFERENCE

And I will pour on the house of David and on the inhabitants of Jerusalem the Spirit of grace and supplication; then they will look on Me whom they have pierced; they will mourn for Him as one mourns for His only Son, and grieve for him as one grieves for a Firstborn. - *Zechariah 12:1*0

Yeshua (Jesus) was also the Firstborn son of the family God chose to bring Him into the world through.

PSALM 22: They Cast Lots for His Clothing

I can count all My bones; [the evildoers] gaze at me. They part my clothing among them, and cast lots for my raiment (a long, shirt-like garment, a seamless* undertunic). - *Psalm 22:17-18*

*Seamless represents eternal - no beginning and no end.

NEW COVENANT REFERENCES

And when they had crucified Him, they divided and distributed His garments [among them] by casting lots so that the prophet's saying was fulfilled, They parted My garments among them and over My apparel they cast lots. - *Matthew 27:35*

And they crucified Him; and they divided His garments and distributed them among themselves, throwing lots for them to decide who should take what. - *Mark 15:24*

Then the soldiers, when they had crucified Jesus, took His garments and made four parts, to each soldier a part, and also the tunic. Now the tunic was without seam, woven from the top in one piece. They said therefore among themselves, "Let us not tear it, but cast lots for it, whose it shall be," that the Scripture might be fulfilled which says:

"They divided My garments among them, and for My clothing they cast lots." - *Yochanan (John) 19:23-24 NKJV*

And Jesus prayed, Father, forgive them, for they know not what they do. And they divided His garments and distributed them by casting lots for them. - *Luke 23:34*

PSALM 22: Atonement, It is Finished

They shall come and shall declare His righteousness to a people yet to be born--that He has done it [that it is finished]! - *Psalm 22:31*

NEW COVENANT REFERENCE

When Jesus had received the sour wine, He said, It is finished! And He bowed His head and gave up His spirit. - *Yochanan (John) 19:30*

Our Salvation was completely accomplished by Yeshua (Jesus) on the Cross. As the Lamb of God, His Blood paid for our sins forever.

PSALM 25: The Secret of His Covenant

The secret [of the sweet, satisfying companionship] of the Lord have they who fear (revere and worship) Him, and He will show them His covenant and reveal to them its [deep, inner] meaning. - *Psalm 25:14*

NEW COVENANT REFERENCES

If any man desires to do His will (God's pleasure), he will know (have the needed illumination to recognize, and can tell for himself) whether the teaching is from God or whether I am speaking from Myself and of My own accord and on My own authority. - *Yochanan (John) 7:17*

I do not call you servants (slaves) any longer, for the servant does not know what his master is doing (working out). But I have called you My friends, because I have made known to you everything that I have heard from My Father, [I have revealed to you everything that I have learned from Him.] - *Yochanan (John) 15:15*

PSALM 31: Into God's Hand, He Commits His Spirit

Into Your hands I commit my spirit; You have redeemed me, O Lord, the God of truth and faithfulness. - *Psalm 31:5*

NEW COVENANT REFERENCE

And Yeshua (Jesus), crying out with a loud voice, said, Father, into Your hands I commit My spirit! And with these words, He expired. - *Luke 23:46*

Being God the Son, Yeshua (Jesus) had power to give His life into the hands of God the Father.

Psalm 40: Messiah Written of In the Volume of the Book

Many, O Lord my God, are the wonderful works which You have done, and your thoughts toward us; no one can compare with You! If I should declare and speak of them, they are too many to be numbered.

Sacrifice and offering You do not desire, nor have You delight in them; You have given me the capacity to hear and obey [Your law, a more valuable service than] burnt offerings and sin offerings [which] You do not require.

Then said I, Behold, I come; in the volume of the book it is written of me; I delight to do Your will, O my God; yes, Your law is within my heart.

I have proclaimed glad tidings of righteousness in the great assembly [tidings of uprightness and right standing with God]; Behold, I have not restrained my lips, as You know, O Lord. - *Psalm 40:5-9**

NEW COVENANT REFERENCE

Hence, when He [Christ] entered into the world, He said, Sacrifices and offerings You have not desired, but instead You have made ready a body for Me [to offer];

In burnt offerings and sin offerings You have taken no delight.

Then I said, Behold, here I am, coming to do Your will, O God--[to fulfill] what is written of Me in the volume of the Book.

When He said just before, You have neither desired, nor have You taken delight in sacrifices and offerings and burnt offerings and sin offerings--all of which are offered according to the Law--

He then went on to say, Behold, [here] I am, coming to do Your will. Thus He does away with and annuls the first (former) order [as a means of expiating sin] so that He might inaugurate and establish the second (latter) order. - *Hebrews 10:5-9**

*It is interesting to note that both the Tanakh and New Covenant references are in verses 5-9.

PSALM 41: The Betrayal of Messiah Yeshua

Even my own familiar friend, in whom I trusted (relied on and was confident), who ate of my bread, has lifted up his heel against me. - *Psalm 41:9*

NEW COVENANT REFERENCES

I am not speaking of and I do not mean all of you. I know whom I have chosen; but it is that the Scripture may be fulfilled, "he who eats My bread with Me has raised up his heel against Me. - *Yochanan (John) 13:18*

Then one of the twelve, call Judas Iscariot, went to the chief priests, and said to them, what will you give me, and I will deliver Him to you? And they covenanted with him for thirty pieces of silver. - *Matthew 26:15*

TANAKH REFERENCE

And I said to them, if you think good, give me my price; and if not, forbear. So they weighed for my price thirty pieces of silver. - *Zechariah 11:12*

In the Scriptures, silver is symbolic of Redemption. Yeshua willingly laid down His life for us. The perfect spotless Lamb of God, Who takes away the sins of the world.

PSALM 45: The Son is God

Thou art fairer than the children of men; Grace is poured into Thy lips; therefore God has blessed Thee forever. Gird Thy sword upon Thy thigh, O Most Mighty, with Thy glory and Thy majesty. And in Thy majesty ride prosperously because of truth and meekness and righteousness ... Thy throne, O God, is for ever and ever: the scepter of Thy kingdom is a right scepter. - *Psalm 45:2-4, 6 KJV*

NEW COVENANT REFERENCE

But to the Son He says, "Thy throne, O God, is for ever and ever: a scepter of righteousness is the scepter of Thy kingdom." - *Hebrews 1:8 KJV*

PSALM 68: He Ascended and Led Captive the Foes

You have ascended on high. You have led away captive a train of vanquished foes; You have received gifts of men, yes, of the rebellious also, that the Lord God might dwell there with them. - *Psalm 68:18*

NEW COVENANT REFERENCES

And yet no one has ever gone up to heaven, but there is One Who has come down from heaven--the Son of Man [Himself], Who is (dwells, has His home) in Heaven. - *Yochanan (John) 3:13*

Therefore it is said, When He ascended on high, He led captivity captive [He led a train of vanquished foes] and He bestowed gifts on men.

[But He ascended] Now what can this, He ascended, mean but that He had previously descended from [the heights of] heaven into [the depths], the lower parts of the earth?

He Who descended is the [very] same as He Who also has ascended high above all the heavens, that He [His presence] might fill all things (the whole universe, from the lowest to the highest).

And His gifts were [varied; He Himself appointed and gave men to us] some to be apostles (special messengers), some prophets (inspired preachers and expounders), some evangelists (preachers of the Gospel, traveling missionaries), some pastors (shepherds of His flock) and teachers...

Rather, let our lives lovingly express truth [in all things, speaking truly, dealing truly, living truly]. Enfolded in love, let us grow up in every way and in all things into Him Who is the Head, [even] Christ (the Messiah, the Anointed One). - *Ephesians 4:8-11, 15*

PSALM 69: They Hated Him Without a Cause

Those who hate me without cause are more than the hairs of my head; those who would cut me off and destroy me, being my enemies wrongfully, are many and mighty. I am [forced] to restore what I did not steal. - *Psalm 69:4*

NEW COVENANT REFERENCE

If I had not done (accomplished) among them the works which no one else ever did, they would not be guilty of sin. But [the fact is] now they have both seen [these works] and have hated both Me and My Father. But [this is so] that the word written in their Law might be fulfilled, They hated Me without a cause. - *Yochanan (John) 15:24-25*

PSALM 69: His Brothers Did Not Believe

Because for Your sake I have borne taunt and reproach; confusion and shame have covered my face. I have become a stranger to my brethren, and an alien to my mother's children. - *Psalm 69:7-8*

NEW COVENANT REFERENCE

So His brothers said to Him, Leave here and go into Judea, so that Your disciples [there] may also see the works that You do. [This is no place for You.] For no one does anything in secret when he wishes to be conspicuous and secure publicity. If You [must] do these things [if you must act like this], show Yourself openly and make yourself known to the world! For [even] His brothers did not believe in or adhere to or trust in or rely on Him either. - *Yochanan (John) 7:3-5*

PSALM 69: His Zeal for God's House

For zeal for Your house has eaten me up, and the reproaches and insults of those who reproach and insult You have fallen upon me. - *Psalm 69:9*

NEW COVENANT REFERENCES

Now the Passover of the Jews was approaching, so Jesus went up to Jerusalem. There He found in the temple [enclosure] those who were selling oxen and sheep and doves, and the money changers sitting there [also at their stands]. And having made a lash (a whip) of cords, He drove them all out of the temple [enclosure]-- both the sheep and the oxen--spilling and scattering the brokers' money and upsetting and tossing around their trays (their stands). Then to those who sold the doves He said, Take these things away (out of here)! Make not My Father's house a house of merchandise (a marketplace, a sales shop)!

And His disciples remembered that it is written [in the Holy Scriptures], Zeal (the fervor of love) for Your house will eat Me up. [I will be consumed with jealously for the honor of Your house.] - *Yochanan (John) 2:13-17*

For Christ did not please Himself [gave no thought to His own interests]; but, as it is written, The reproaches and abuses of those who reproached and abused you fell on Me. - *Romans 15:3*

Psalm 69: They Gave Him Vinegar to Drink

They gave me also gall [poisonous and bitter] for My food, and in My thirst they gave Me vinegar (a soured wine) to drink. - *Psalm 69:21*

NEW COVENANT REFERENCES

Before the crucifixion:

They offered Him wine mingled with gall to drink; but when He tasted it, He refused to drink it.

After the crucifixion:

And one of them immediately ran and took a sponge, soaked it with vinegar (a sour wine), and put it on a reed (staff), and was about to give it to Him to drink. - *Matthew 27:34, 48*

And one man ran, and, filling a sponge with vinegar (a mixture of sour wine and water), put it on a staff made of a [bamboo-like] reed and gave it to Him to drink, saying, Hold off! Let us see whether Elijah [does] come to take Him down. - *Mark 15:36*

The soldiers also ridiculed and made sport of Him, coming up and offering Him vinegar (a sour wine mixed with water). - *Luke 23:36*

PSALMS 72 and 76: Gifts for the King of Kings

10 The kings of Tarshish and of the isles shall bring presents: the kings of Sheba and seba shall offer gifts...15 And He shall live, and to Him shall be given of the gold of Sheba; - *Psalm 72:10, 15*

Verse 15 of this Psalm is also prophetic in saying "He shall live". Shortly after the wise men visited the Messiah, Herod brought forth a decree to have every male child age two and under put to death in Bethlehem (Matt. 2:16). Jesus escaped this when they fled to Egypt.

Vow and pay to the LORD your God; let all who are round about Him bring presents to Him Who ought to be [reverently] feared. - *Psalm 76:11*

NEW COVENANT REFERENCE

And on going into the house, they (the wise men) saw the Child with Mary His mother, and they fell down and worshiped Him. Then opening their treasure bags, they presented to Him gifts--gold and frankincense and myrrh. - *Matthew 2:11*

The gifts the wise men brought to Yeshua (Jesus) when He was a child were prophetically symbolic: Gold, for Kingship; Frankincense, for Priesthood; and Myrrh, for sacrifice.

It is interesting to note that the prophetic verse from Psalm 76 and it's fulfillment in the Gospel of Matthew are both verse 11.

TANAKH REFERENCE

A multitude of camels [from the eastern trading tribes] shall cover you [Jerusalem], the young camels of Midian and Ephah; all the men from Sheba [who once came to trade] shall come, bringing gold and frankincense and proclaiming the praises of the Lord. - *Isaiah 60:6*

PSALM 76: He Cut Off the Spirit of Princes

He will cut off the spirit [of pride and fury] of princes; He is terrible to the [ungodly] kings of the earth. - *Psalm 76:12*

NEW COVENANT REFERENCE

[God] disarmed the principalities and powers that were ranged against us and made a bold display and public example of them, in triumphing over them in Him and in it [the cross]. - *Colossians 2:15*

By Atoning for us with the shedding of His Divine Blood, Yeshua (Jesus) also defeated the powers of darkness, having completely disarmed them from any spiritual power or dominion over us who believe.

TANAKH REFERENCE

Lord, You will ordain peace (God's favor and blessings, both temporal and spiritual) for us, for You have also wrought in us and for us all our works.

O Lord, our God, other masters besides You have ruled over us, but we will acknowledge and mention Your name only.

They [the former tyrant masters] are dead, they shall not live and reappear; they are powerless ghosts, they shall not rise and come back. Therefore You have visited and made an end of them and caused every memory of them [every trace of their supremacy] to perish. - *Isaiah 26:12-14*

The Scripture in Isaiah 26 says "You will ordain peace for us". At that time, this denoted a deliverance to come (prophesied about).

PSALM 78: He Taught in Parables

I will open my mouth in a parable (in instruction by numerous examples); I will utter dark sayings of old [that hide important truth]. - *Psalm 78:2*

NEW COVENANT REFERENCES

These things all taken together Jesus said to the crowds in parables; indeed, without a parable He said nothing to them. This was in fulfillment of what was spoken by the prophet: I will open My mouth in parables; I will utter things that have been hidden since the foundation of the world. - *Matthew 13:34-35*

Then the disciples came to Him and said, Why do You speak to them in parables?

And He replied to them, To you it has been given to know the secrets and mysteries of the kingdom of heaven, but to them it has not been given.

For whoever has [spiritual knowledge], to him will more be given and he will be furnished richly so that he will have abundance; but from him who has not, even what he has will be taken away.

This is the reason that I speak to them in parables: because having the power of seeing, they do not see; and having the power of hearing, they do not hear, nor do they grasp and understand. - *Matthew 13:10-13*

The words of a [discreet and wise] man's mouth are like deep waters [plenteous and difficult to fathom], and the fountain of skillful and godly Wisdom is like a gushing stream [sparkling, fresh, pure, and life-giving].
–Proverbs 18:4

PSALM 89: The Firstborn

Also I will make Him the Firstborn, the Highest of the kings of the earth.
- *Psalm 89:27*

NEW COVENANT REFERENCES

And from Jesus Christ the faithful and trustworthy Witness, the First-born of the dead [first to be brought back to life] and the Prince (Ruler) of the kings of the earth. To Him Who ever loves us and has once [for all] loosed and freed us from our sins by His own Blood. - *Revelation 1:5*

For those whom He foreknew [of whom He was aware and loved before-hand], He also destined from the beginning [foreordaining them] to be molded into the image of His Son [and share inwardly His likeness], that He might become the firstborn among many brethren. - *Romans 8:29*

In Whom we have our redemption through His blood, [which means] the forgiveness of our sins. [Now] He is the exact likeness of the unseen God [the visible representation of the invisible]; He is the Firstborn of all creation. - *Colossians 1:14-15*

He also is the Head of [His] body, the church; seeing He is the Begin-ning, the Firstborn from among the dead, so that He alone in everything and in every respect might occupy the chief place [stand first and be preeminent]. For it has pleased [the Father] that all the divine fullness (the sum total of the divine perfection, powers, and attributes) should dwell in Him permanently. - *Colossians 1:18-19*

Messiah Yeshua (Jesus) is called "Firstborn" from the dead. He is God the Son and the Word made flesh that came and dwelt among us. All who receive Him become reborn in their spirit, as GOD is a Spirit and He has spiritual offspring.

PSALM 107: The Word Sent Forth

He sends forth His word and heals them and rescues them from the pit and destruction. - *Psalm 107:20*

NEW COVENANT REFERENCES

As Jesus went into Capernaum, a centurion came up to Him, begging Him, and saying, Lord, my servant boy is lying at the house paralyzed and distressed with intense pains. And Jesus said to him, I will come and restore him. But the centurion replied to Him, Lord, I am not worthy to have You come under my roof, but only speak the word, and my servant boy will be cured. - *Matthew 8:8*

In the beginning was the Word, and the Word was with God, and the Word was God. - *Yochanan (John) 1:1*

He is dressed in a robe dyed by dipping in blood, and the title by which He is called is The Word of God. - *Revelation 19:13*

TANAKH REFERENCE

Who has ascended into heaven and descended? Who has gathered the wind in His fists? Who has bound the waters in His garment? Who has established all the ends of the earth? What is His name, and what is His Son's name, if you know?

Every word of God is tried and purified; He is a shield to those who trust and take refuge in Him. - *Proverbs 30:4-5*

PSALM 107: He Calmed the Storm

Then they cry to the Lord in their trouble, and He brings them out of their distresses. He hushes the storm to a calm and to a gentle whisper, so that the waves of the sea are still. Then the men are glad because of the calm, and He brings them to their desired haven. - *Psalm 107:28-30*

See how the verses of Scripture in Psalm 107 correspond to what happened in Matthew 8. First they cry for help, and He calms the storm. Then they marvel.

NEW COVENANT REFERENCE

And after He got into the boat, His disciples followed Him. And suddenly, behold, there arose a violent storm on the sea, so that the boat was being covered up by the waves; but He was sleeping.

And they went and awakened Him, saying, Lord, rescue and preserve us! We are perishing!

And He said to them, Why are you timid and afraid, O you of little faith? Then He got up and rebuked the winds and the sea, and there was a great and wonderful calm (a perfect peaceableness). And the men were stunned with bewildered wonder and marveled, saying, What kind of Man is this, that even the winds and the sea obey Him! - *Matthew 8:23-27*

PSALM 110: The LORD Said to My Lord (Father & Son)

The LORD (God) says to my Lord (the Messiah), Sit at My right hand, until I make Your adversaries Your footstool. - *Psalm 110:1*

The all capitals "LORD" in the Hebrew is "Yahweh" and "Lord" is "Adonai".

NEW COVENANT REFERENCES

And as Jesus taught in [a porch or court of] the temple, He said, How can the scribes say that the Christ is David's Son? David himself [inspired] in the Holy Spirit, declared, The Lord said to my Lord, Sit at My right hand until I make Your enemies [a footstool] under Your feet. - *Mark 12:36*

For David did not ascend into the heavens; yet he himself says, The LORD said to my Lord, Sit at My right hand and share My throne until I make Your enemies a footstool for Your feet. - *Acts 2:34-35*

For [Christ] must be King and reign until He has put all [His] enemies under His feet. - *I Corinthians 15:25*

If then you have been raised with Christ [to a new life, thus sharing His resurrection from the dead], aim at and seek the [rich, eternal treasures] that are above, where Christ is, seated at the right hand of God.
- Colossians 3:1

Whereas this One [Christ], after He had offered a single sacrifice for our sins [that shall avail] for all time, sat down at the right hand of God, Then to wait until His enemies should be made a stool beneath His feet.
- Hebrews 10:12-13

Looking away [from all that will distract] to Jesus, Who is the Leader and the Source of our faith [giving the first incentive for our belief] and is also its Finisher [bringing it to maturity and perfection]. He, for the joy [of obtaining the prize] that was set before Him, endured the cross, despising and ignoring the shame, and is now seated at the right hand of the throne of God. *- Hebrews 12:2*

TANAKH REFERENCE

I saw in the night visions, and behold, on the clouds of the heavens came One like a Son of man, and He came to the Ancient of Days and was presented before Him. *- Daniel 7:13*

PSALM 110: Messiah's Eternal Priesthood

The LORD has sworn and will not revoke or change it: You are a priest forever, after the manner and order of Melchizedek. - *Psalm 110:4*

NEW COVENANT REFERENCES

Being designated and recognized and saluted by God as High Priest after the order (with the rank) of Melchizedek. - *Hebrews 5:10*

Now if perfection (a perfect fellowship between God and the worshiper) had been attainable by the Levitical priesthood--for under it the people were given the Law--why was it further necessary that there should arise another and different kind of Priest, one after the order of Melchizedek, rather than one appointed after the order and rank of Aaron? - *Hebrews 7:11*

For it is obvious that our Lord sprang from the tribe of Judah, and Moses mentioned nothing about priests in connection with that tribe.

And this becomes more plainly evident when another Priest arises Who bears the likeness of Melchizedek. - *Hebrews 7:14-15*

For those who formerly became priests received their office without its being confirmed by the taking of an oath by God, but this One was designated and addressed and saluted with an oath, The Lord has sworn and will not regret it or change His mind, You are a Priest forever according to the order of Melchizedek. - *Hebrews 7:21*

At this the people answered Him. We have learned from the Law that the Christ is to remain forever. - *John 12:34a*

PSALM 118: The Chief Cornerstone

This is the gate of the LORD; the [uncompromisingly] righteous shall enter through it.

I will confess, praise, and give thanks to You, for You have heard and answered me; and You have become my Salvation and Deliverer.

The stone which the builders rejected has become the chief cornerstone. This is from the LORD and is His doing; it is marvelous in our eyes.
- *Psalm 118:20-23*

These Scriptures are written within the context of Salvation. Yeshua (Jesus) is the Door (the Way we enter in). Therefore "the gate of the LORD" refers to Him. So the three verses tie together the Gate (Way), the Lord being our Salvation and Deliverer and the stone that was rejected yet is the Head Cornerstone.

NEW COVENANT REFERENCES

Jesus asked them, Have you never read in the Scriptures: The very Stone which the builders rejected and threw away has become the Cornerstone; this is the Lord's doing, and it is marvelous in our eyes? - *Matthew 21:42*

I am the door. If anyone enters by Me, he will be saved, and will go in and out and find pasture. - *John 10:9*

Have you not even read this [passage of] Scripture: The very Stone which [after putting it to the test] the builders rejected has become the Head of the corner [Cornerstone]; This is from the LORD and is His doing and it is marvelous in our eyes. - *Mark 12:1-11*

PSALM 118: Messiah's Triumphant Entry Into Jerusalem

Save now, we beseech You, O Lord;

Blessed is He who comes in the name of the Lord; we bless you from the house of the LORD [you who come into His sanctuary under His guardianship].

The LORD is God, Who has shown and given us light [He has illuminated us with grace, freedom, and joy]. Decorate the festival with leafy boughs and bind the sacrifices to be offered with thick cords [all over the priest's court, right up] to the horns of the altar. - *Psalm 118:25-27*

Psalm 118 was prophetic in speaking of Messiah Yeshua's triumphant entry into Jerusalem: Save now, Blessed is He..., decorate the festival with leafy boughs and bind the sacrifice to be offered. This is a picture of Yeshua being our Salvation; being heralded by the people with the palm branches, and all this before His life was offered up a sacrifice for our sins.

NEW COVENANT REFERENCE

And many [of the people] spread their garments on the road, and others [scattered a layer of] leafy branches which they had cut from the fields.

And those who went before and those who followed cried out [with a cry of happiness], Hosanna! [Be graciously inclined and propitious to Him!] Praised and blessed is He Who comes in the name of the LORD!

Praised and blessed in the name of the Lord is the coming kingdom of our father David! Hosanna (O save us) in the highest [heaven]! - *Mark 11:8-10*

PSALM 132: Messiah Set Upon the Throne of David

The Lord swore to David in truth; He will not turn back from it: One of the fruit of your body I will set upon your throne. - *Psalm 132:11*

NEW COVENANT REFERENCES

THE BOOK of the ancestry (genealogy) of Jesus Christ (the Messiah, the Anointed), the son (descendant) of David, the son (descendant) of Abraham. - *Matthew 1:1*

He will be great (eminent) and will be called the Son of the Most High; and the Lord God will give to Him the throne of His forefather David, And He will reign over the house of Jacob throughout the ages; and of His reign there will be no end. - *Luke 1:32-33*

And He has raised up a Horn of salvation [a mighty and valiant Helper, the Author of salvation] for us in the house of David His servant--

This is as He promised by the mouth of His holy prophets from the most ancient times [in the memory of man] - *Luke 1:69-70*

(King David) Being however a prophet, and knowing that God had sealed to him with an oath that He would set one of his descendants on his throne. - *Acts 2:30*

TANAKH REFERENCES

[You have said] I have made a covenant with My chosen one, I have sworn to David My servant, Your Seed I will establish forever, and I will build up your throne for all generations. Selah [pause, and calmly think of that]! - *Psalm 89:3-4*

Of the increase of His government and of peace there shall be no end, upon the throne of David and over his kingdom, to establish it and to uphold it with justice and with righteousness from the [latter] time forth, even forevermore. The zeal of the Lord of hosts will perform this. - *Isaiah 9:7*

PROVERBS: What is His Son's Name?
A Riddle Revealed

Who has ascended up into heaven, or descended? Who has gathered the wind in His fists? Who has bound the waters in a garment? Who has established all the ends of the earth? What is His name, and what is His son's name, if you know?

Every Word of God is pure: He is a shield to those who put their trust in Him. - *Proverbs 30:4-5 NKJV*

The answer to the question in verse 4 is found immediately in verse 5. Verse 5 refers to "Word of God" as "He" and "Him."

NEW COVENANT REFERENCES

In the beginning was the Word, and the Word was with God, and the Word was God. - *Yochanan (John) 1:1*

And yet no one has ever gone up to heaven, but there is One Who has come down from heaven--the Son of Man [Himself], Who is (dwells, has His home) in heaven. - *Yochanan (John) 3:13*

Now I saw heaven opened, and behold, a white horse. And He who sat on him was called Faithful and True, and in righteousness He judges and makes war.

His eyes were like a flame of fire, and on His head were many crowns. He had a name written that no one knew except Himself.

He was clothed with a robe dipped in blood, and His name is called the Word of God. - *Revelation 19:11-13 NKJV*

SONG OF SOLOMON: Love that Conquered Death

Set me like a seal upon your heart, like a seal upon your arm; for love is as strong as death, jealously is as hard and cruel as Sheol (the place of the dead). Its flashes are flashes of fire, a most vehement flame [the very flame of the LORD]!

Many waters cannot quench love, neither can floods drown it. If a man would offer all the goods of his house for love, he would be utterly scorned and despised. - *Song of Solomon 8:6-7*

Yeshua (Jesus) gave up His life for us on the Cross for the sins of the whole world. He is our Redeemer. He conquered death for us and rose from the tomb. The prophetic verses in Song of Solomon prophetically portrays this Love, that would give His Life for us.

NEW COVENANT REFERENCE

No one has greater love [no one has shown stronger affection] than to lay down (give up) his own life for his friends. - *Yochanan (John) 15:13*

TANAKH REFERENCES

For the LORD your God is a consuming fire, a jealous God.
- *Deuteronomy 4:24*

He was despised and rejected and forsaken by men, a Man of sorrows and pains, and acquainted with grief and sickness; and like One from Whom men hide their faces He was despised, and we did not appreciate His worth or have any esteem for Him. - *Isaiah 53:3*

The Prophets

ISAIAH: Messiah Born of a Virgin

Therefore the Lord Himself shall give you a sign: Behold, the young woman who is unmarried and a virgin shall conceive and bear a Son, and shall call His name Immanuel [God with us]. - *Isaiah 7:14*

The name "Isaiah" means "The Salvation of God". The book of Isaiah is the most Messianic prophetic book in the entire Tanakh.

NEW COVENANT REFERENCES

Now the birth of Jesus Christ took place under these circumstances: When His mother Mary had been promised in marriage to Joseph, before they came together, she was found to be pregnant [through the power] of the Holy Spirit.

And her [promised] husband Joseph, being a just and upright man and not willing to expose her publicly and to shame and disgrace her, decided to repudiate and dismiss (divorce) her quietly and secretly.

But as he was thinking this over, behold, an angel of the Lord appeared to him in a dream, saying, Joseph, descendant of David, do not be afraid to take Mary [as] your wife, for that which is conceived in her is of (from, out of) the Holy Spirit.

She will bear a Son, and you shall call His name Jesus [the Greek form of the Hebrew Joshua, which means Savior], for He will save His people from their sins [that is, prevent them from failing and missing the true end and scope of life, which is God].

All this took place that it might be fulfilled which the Lord had spoken through the prophet,

Behold, the virgin shall become pregnant and give birth to a Son, and they shall call His name Emmanuel--which, when translated, means, God with us.

Then Joseph, being aroused from his sleep, did as the angel of the Lord had commanded him: he took [her to his side as] his wife.

But he had no union with her as her husband until she had borne her firstborn Son; and he called His name Jesus. - *Matthew 1:18-25*

Then the angel said to her, The Holy Spirit will come upon you, and the power of the Most High will overshadow you [like a shining cloud]; and so the holy (pure, sinless) Thing (Offspring) which shall be born of you will be called the Son of God. - *Luke 1:35*

ISAIAH: He Shall Be a Stone and a Rock of Offense

And He shall be a sanctuary [a sacred and indestructible asylum to those who reverently fear and trust in Him]; but He shall be a Stone of stumbling and a Rock of offense to both the houses of Israel, a trap and a snare to the inhabitants of Jerusalem. - *Isaiah 8:14-15*

This is a hard passage. Isaiah in his day, spoke of One to come ("He shall be..."). The only way this can be truly understood is to look at the New Covenant references from the B'rit Hadashah:

NEW COVENANT REFERENCES

And Simeon blessed them and said to Mary His mother, Behold, This Child is appointed and destined for the fall and rising of many in Israel, and for a sign that is spoken against. - *Luke 2:34*

Whereas Israel, though ever in pursuit of a law [for the securing] of righteousness (right standing with God), actually did not succeed in fulfilling the Law.

For what reason? Because [they pursued it] not through faith, relying [instead] on the merit of their works [they did not depend on faith but on what they could do]. They have stumbled over the Stumbling Stone.

As it is written, Behold I am laying in Zion a Stone that will make men stumble, a Rock that will make them fall; but he who believes in Him [who adheres to, trusts in, and relies on Him] shall not be put to shame nor be disappointed in his expectations. - *Romans 9:31-33*

For thus it stands in Scripture: Behold, I am laying in Zion a chosen (honored), precious chief Cornerstone, and he who believes in Him [who adheres to, trusts in, and relies on Him] shall never be disappointed or put to shame.

To you then who believe (who adhere to, trust in, and rely on Him) is the preciousness; but for those who disbelieve [it is true], The [very] Stone which the builders rejected has become the main Cornerstone. (see also Psalm 118:22)

And, A Stone that will cause stumbling and a Rock that will give [men] offense; they stumble because they disobey and disbelieve [God's] Word, as those [who reject Him] were destined (appointed) to do.

But you are a chosen race, a royal priesthood, a dedicated nation, [God's] own purchased, special people, that you may set forth the wonderful deeds and display the virtues and perfections of Him Who called you out of darkness into His marvelous light. - *I Peter 2:6-9*

ISAIAH: A Son is Given

For to us a Child is born, to us a Son is given; and the government shall be upon His shoulder, and His name shall be called Wonderful Counselor, Mighty God, Everlasting Father [of Eternity] Prince of Peace.
- *Isaiah 9:6*

This prophecy speaks of a Child born - a Son, Who is God and Everlasting Father.

NEW COVENANT REFERENCES

And Joseph also went up from Galilee from the town of Nazareth to Judea, to the town of David, which is called Bethlehem, because he was of the house and family of David ...

And while they were there, the time came for her delivery, and she gave birth to her Son, her Firstborn; and she wrapped Him in swaddling clothes and laid Him in a manger, because there was no room or place for them in the inn.

And in that vicinity there were shepherds living [out under the open sky] in the field, watching [in shifts] over their flock by night.

And behold, an angel of the Lord stood by them, and the glory of the Lord flashed and shone all about them, and they were terribly frightened.

But the Angel said to them, Do not be afraid; for behold, I bring you good news of a great joy which will come to all the people.

For to you is born this day in the town of David a Savior, Who is Christ (the Messiah) the Lord!...

And at the end of eight days, when [the Baby] was to be circumcised, He was called Jesus (Yeshua), the name given by the angel before He was conceived in the womb. - *Luke 2:4, 6-11, 21*

Jesus approached and, breaking the silence, said to them, All authority (all power of rule) in heaven and on earth has been given to Me. - *Matthew 28:18*

ISAIAH: He Shall Be a Nazarene (Branch: Separated One)

And there shall come forth a Shoot out of the stock of Jesse [David's father], and a Branch out of his roots shall grow and bear fruit. - *Isaiah 11:1*

NEW COVENANT REFERENCES

He went and dwelt in a town called Nazareth, so that what was spoken through the prophets might be fulfilled: He shall be called a Nazarene [Branch, Separated One]. - *Matthew 2:23*

I, Jesus, have sent My messenger (angel) to you to witness and to give you assurance of these things for the churches (assemblies). I am the Root (and Source) and the Offspring of David, the radiant and brilliant Morning Star. - *Revelation 22:16*

TANAKH REFERENCE

And the Lord said to Moses, Say to the Israelites, When either a man or a woman shall make a special vow, the vow of a Nazarite, that is, one separated and consecrated to the Lord. - *Numbers 6:1*

ISAIAH: From the Stock of Jesse (King David's Father)

And there shall come forth a Shoot out of the stock of Jesse [David's father], and a Branch out of his roots shall grow and bear fruit.

And the Spirit of the Lord shall rest upon Him--the Spirit of wisdom and understanding, the Spirit of counsel and might, the Spirit of knowledge and of the reverential and obedient fear of the Lord. - *Isaiah 11:1-2*

NEW COVENANT REFERENCES

THE BOOK of the ancestry (genealogy) of Jesus Christ (the Messiah, the Anointed), the son (descendant) of David, the son (descendant) of Abraham. - *Matthew 1:1*

And Joseph also went up from Galilee from the town of Nazareth to Judea, to the town of David, which is called Bethlehem, because he was of the house and family of David, to be enrolled with Mary, his espoused (married) wife, who was about to become a mother. - *Luke 2:4-5*

ISAIAH: He Shall Stand as a Signal (Sign)

And it shall be in that day that the Root of Jesse shall stand as a signal for the peoples; of Him shall the nations inquire and seek knowledge, and His dwelling shall be glory [His rest glorious]! - *Isaiah 11:10*

NEW COVENANT REFERENCE

And I, if and when I am lifted up from the earth [on the cross], will draw and attract all men [Gentiles as well as Jews] to Myself. - *John 12:32*

ISAIAH: Wells of Salvation, Living Water

And in that day you will say, I will give thanks to You, O Lord; for though You were angry with me, Your anger has turned away, and You comfort me.

Behold, God, my Salvation! I will trust and not be afraid, for the Lord God is my strength and song; yes, He has become my Salvation.

Therefore with joy will you draw water from the wells of Salvation.

And in that day you will say, Give thanks to the Lord, call upon His name and by means of His name [in solemn entreaty] declare and make known His deeds among the peoples of the earth, proclaim that His name is exalted!

Sing praises to the Lord, for He has done excellent things [gloriously]; let this be made known to all the earth.

Cry aloud and shout joyfully, you women and inhabitants of Zion, for great in your midst is the Holy One of Israel. - *Isaiah 12*

NEW COVENANT REFERENCE

...He arrived at a Samaritan town called Sychar, near the tract of land that Jacob gave to his son Joseph.

And Jacob's well was there. So Jesus, tired as He was from His journey, sat down [to rest] by the well. It was then about the sixth hour (about noon).

Presently, when a woman of Samaria came along to draw water, Jesus said to her, Give Me a drink--...

The Samaritan woman said to Him, How is it that You, being a Jew, ask me, a Samaritan [and a] woman, for a drink?--For the Jews have nothing to do with the Samaritans--

Jesus answered her, If you had only known and had recognized God's gift and Who this is that is saying to you, Give Me a drink, you would have asked Him [instead] and He would have given you Living Water.

She said to Him, Sir, You have nothing to draw with [no drawing bucket] and the well is deep; how then can You provide living water? [Where do You get Your living water?]

Are you greater than and superior to our ancestor Jacob, who gave us this well and who used to drink from it himself, and his sons and his cattle also?

Jesus answered her, All who drink of this water will be thirsty again. But whoever takes a drink of the water that I will give him shall never, no never, be thirsty anymore. But the water that I will give him shall become a spring of water welling up (flowing, bubbling) [continually] within him unto (into, for) eternal life.

The woman said to Him, Sir, give me this water, so that I may never get thirsty nor have to come [continually all the way] here to draw.

At this, Jesus said to her, Go, call your husband and come back here.

The woman answered, I have no husband. Jesus said to her, you have spoken truly in saying, I have no husband.

For you have had five husbands, and the man you are now living with is not your husband. In this you have spoken truly.

The woman said to Him, Sir, I see and understand that You are a prophet.

Our forefathers worshiped on this mountain, but you [Jews] say that Jerusalem is the place where it is necessary and proper to worship.

Jesus said to her, Woman, believe Me, a time is coming when you will worship the Father neither [merely] in this mountain nor [merely] in Jerusalem.

You [Samaritans] do not know what you are worshiping [you worship what you do not comprehend]. We do know what we are worshiping [we worship what we have knowledge of and understand], for [after all] salvation comes from [among] the Jews.

A time will come, however, indeed it is already here, when the true (genuine) worshipers will worship the Father in spirit and in truth (reality); for the Father is seeking just such people as these as His worshipers.

God is a Spirit (a spiritual Being) and those who worship Him must worship Him in spirit and in truth (reality).

The woman said to Him, I know that Messiah is coming, He Who is called the Christ (the Anointed One); and when He arrives, He will tell us everything we need to know and make it clear to us.

Jesus said to her, I Who now speak with you am He. - *Yochanan (John) 4:5-26*

ISAIAH: Messiah Yeshua Has the Key of David

And the key of the house of David I will lay upon His shoulder; He shall open and no one shall shut, He shall shut and no one shall open. - *Isaiah 22:22*

And I will fasten Him like a peg or nail in a firm place; and He will become a throne of honor and glory to His Father's house.

And they will hang on Him the honor and the whole weight of [responsibility for] His Father's house: the offspring and issue [of the family, high and low], every small vessel, from the cups even to all the flasks and big bulging bottles.

In that day, says the Lord of hosts, the nail or peg that was fastened into the sure place shall give way and be moved and be hewn down and fall, and the burden that was upon it shall be cut off; for the Lord has spoken it. - *Isaiah 22:23-25*

God laid the cross upon Yeshua's (Jesus) shoulder to bear our sins upon it. He was nailed to that cross (fastened like a peg or nail). Pilate had a sign hung on that cross that said: JESUS OF NAZARETH, THE KING OF THE JEWS *(See John 19:19)*.

NEW COVENANT REFERENCE

And to the angel (messenger) of the assembly (church) in Philadelphia write: These are the words of the Holy One, the True One, He Who has the key of David, Who opens and no one shall shut, Who shuts and no one shall open. - *Revelation 3:7*

ISAIAH: He Swallowed Up Death In Victory

He will swallow up death [in Victory; He will abolish death forever]. And the Lord God will wipe away tears from all faces; and the reproach of His people He will take away from off all the earth; for the Lord has spoken it.

It shall be said in that day, Behold our God upon Whom we have waited and hoped, that He might save us! This is the Lord, we have waited for Him; we will be glad and rejoice in His Salvation. - *Isaiah 25:8-9*

NEW COVENANT REFERENCES

For [Christ] must be King and reign until He has put all [His] enemies under His feet. The last enemy to be subdued and abolished is death. - *I Corinthians 15:25-26*

And when this perishable puts on the imperishable and this that was capable of dying puts on freedom from death, then shall be fulfilled the Scripture that says, Death is swallowed up (utterly vanquished forever) in and unto victory. - *I Corinthians 15:54*

[It is that purpose and grace] which He now has made known and has fully disclosed and made real [to us] through the appearing of our Savior Christ Jesus, Who annulled death and made it of no effect and brought life and immortality (immunity from eternal death) to light through the Gospel. - *2 Timothy 1:10*

ISAIAH: Messiah, a Foundation Stone

Therefore thus says the LORD God, Behold, I am laying in Zion for a foundation a Stone, a tested Stone, a precious Cornerstone of sure foundation; he who believes (trusts in, relies on, and adheres to that Stone) will not be ashamed or give way or hasten away [in sudden panic].
- *Isaiah 28:16*

NEW COVENANT REFERENCES

Jesus asked them, Have you never read in the Scriptures: The very Stone which the builders rejected and threw away has become the Cornerstone; this is the Lord's doing, and it is marvelous in our eyes? - *Matthew 21:42*

This [Jesus] is the Stone which was despised and rejected by you, the builders, but which has become the Head of the corner [the Cornerstone].

And there is Salvation in and through no one else, for there is no other Name under heaven given among men by and in which we must be saved.
- *Acts 4:11-12*

As it is written, Behold I am laying in Zion a Stone that will make men stumble, a Rock that will make them fall; but he who believes in Him [who adheres to, trusts in, and relies on Him] shall not be put to shame nor be disappointed in his expectations. - *Romans 9:33*

You are built upon the foundation of the apostles and prophets with Christ Jesus Himself the chief Cornerstone. - *Ephesians 2:20*

Come to Him [then, to that] Living Stone which men tried and threw away, but which is chosen [and] precious in God's sight. - *I Peter 2:4*

ISAIAH: The Kingdom of God Has Come to You

Then the eyes of the blind shall be opened, and the ears of the deaf shall be unstopped. Then shall the lame man leap like a hart, and the tongue of the dumb shall sing for joy. For waters shall break forth in the wilderness and streams in the desert. - *Isaiah 35:5-6*

NEW COVENANT REFERENCE

Now when John in prison heard about the activities of Christ, he sent a message by his disciples and asked Him, Are You the One Who was to come, or should we keep on expecting a different one?

And Jesus replied to them, Go and report to John what you hear and see:

The blind receive their sight and the lame walk, lepers are cleansed (by healing) and the deaf hear, the dead are raised up and the poor have good news (the Gospel) preached to them. - *Matthew 11:2-5*

ISAIAH: The Glory of the Lord Is Revealed

And the glory (majesty and splendor) of the Lord shall be revealed, and all flesh shall see it together; for the mouth of the Lord has spoken it.
- Isaiah 40:5

NEW COVENANT REFERENCES

And the Word (Christ) became flesh (human, incarnate) and tabernacled (fixed His tent of flesh, lived awhile) among us; and we [actually] saw His glory (His honor, His majesty), such glory as an only begotten son receives from His father, full of grace (favor, loving-kindness) and truth.
- Yochanan (John) 1:14

And all mankind shall see (behold and understand and at last acknowledge) the Salvation of God (the deliverance from eternal death decreed by God). *- Luke 3:6*

ISAIAH: Behold My Servant

Behold My Servant, Whom I uphold, My elect in Whom My soul delights! I have put My Spirit upon Him; He will Bring forth justice and right and reveal truth to the nations. - *Isaiah 42:1*

NEW COVENANT REFERENCE

And when Jesus was baptized, He went up at once out of the water; and behold, the heavens were opened, and he [John] saw the Spirit of God descending like a dove and alighting on Him.

And behold, a Voice from heaven said, This is My Son, My Beloved, in Whom I delight! - *Matthew 3:16-17*

TANAKH REFERENCE

His eyes are as the eyes of doves by the rivers of waters.
- *Song of Solomon 5:12*

ISAIAH: He will Not Cry Aloud

He will not cry or shout aloud or cause His voice to be heard in the street. A bruised reed He will not break, and a dimly burning wick He will not quench; He will bring forth justice in truth. - *Isaiah 42:2-3*

NEW COVENANT REFERENCE

But the Pharisees went out and held a consultation against Him, how they might do away with Him. But being aware of this, Jesus went away from there. And many people joined and accompanied Him, and He cured all of them.

And strictly charged them and sharply warned them not to make Him publicly known.

This was in fulfillment of what was spoken by the prophet Isaiah,

Behold, My Servant Whom I have chosen. My Beloved in and with Whom My soul is well pleased and has found its delight. I will put My Spirit upon Him, and He shall proclaim and show forth justice to the nations.

He will not strive or wrangle or cry out loudly; nor will anyone hear His voice in the streets; a bruised reed He will not break, and a smoldering (dimly burning) wick He will not quench, till He brings justice and a just cause to victory.

And in and on His name will the Gentiles (the peoples outside of Israel) set their hopes. - *Matthew 12:14-21*

ISAIAH: He Opened the Eyes of the Blind

I the LORD have called You [the Messiah] for a righteous purpose and in righteousness; I will take You by the hand and will keep You; I will give You for a covenant to the people [Israel], for a light to the nations [Gentiles],

To open the eyes of the blind, to bring out prisoners from the dungeon, and those who sit in darkness from the prison. - *Isaiah 42:6-7*

NEW COVENANT REFERENCES

As Jesus passed on from there, two blind men followed Him, shouting loudly, Have pity and mercy on us, Son of David! When He reached the house and went in, the blind men came to Him, and Jesus said to them, Do you believe that I am able to do this? They said to Him, Yes, Lord. Then He touched their eyes, saying, According to your faith and trust and reliance [on the power invested in Me] be it done to you; And their eyes were opened. - *Matthew 9:27-30*

Then a blind and dumb man under the power of a demon was brought to Jesus, and He cured him, so that the blind and dumb man both spoke and saw. - *Matthew 12:22*

AS HE passed along, He noticed a man blind from his birth. His disciples asked Him, Rabbi, who sinned, this man or his parents, that he should be born blind?

Jesus answered, It was not that this man or his parents sinned, but he was born blind in order that the workings of God should be manifested (displayed and illustrated) in him...As long as I am in the world, I am the world's Light.

When He had said this, He spat on the ground and made clay (mud) with His saliva, and He spread it [as ointment] on the man's eyes. And He said to him, Go, wash in the Pool of Siloam---which means Sent. So he went and washed, and came back seeing. - *Yochanan (John) 9:1-7*

TANAKH REFERENCE

Then the Lord God formed man from the dust of the ground and breathed into his nostrils the breath or spirit of life, and the man became a living being. - *Genesis 2:7*

God created man from the soil (dust of the ground). Yeshua (Jesus) healed the blind man's eyes in John 9 using mud.

ISAIAH: The LORD and His Redeemer, First & Last

Thus says the LORD, the King of Israel and His Redeemer, the Lord of hosts: I am the First and I am the Last; besides Me there is no God.
- *Isaiah 44:6*

Another Father and Son Scripture: The LORD, the King of Israel AND His Redeemer, the Lord of hosts.

NEW COVENANT REFERENCES

When I saw Him, I fell at His feet as if dead. But He laid His right hand on me and said, Do not be afraid! I am the First and the Last.
- *Revelation (to Yochanan) 1:17*

And to the angel (messenger) of the assembly (church) in Smyrna write: These are the words of the First and the Last, Who died and came to life again. - *Revelation 2:8*

I am the Alpha and the Omega, the First and the Last (the Before all and the End of all). - *Revelation 22:13*

TANAKH REFERENCES

Who has prepared and done this, calling forth and guiding the destinies of the generations [of the nations] from the beginning? I, the Lord--the first [existing before history began] and with the last [an ever-present, unchanging God--I am He. - *Isaiah 41:4*

Listen to Me, O Jacob, and Israel, My called [ones]: I am He; I am the First, I also am the Last. - *Isaiah 48:12*

ISAIAH: He Did Not Speak in Secret

I have not spoken in secret, in a corner of the land of darkness; I did not call the descendents of Jacob [to a fruitless service], saying, Seek Me for nothing [but I promised them a just reward]. I, the Lord, speak righteousness (the truth--trustworthy, straightforward correspondence between deeds and words); I declare things that are right. - *Isaiah 45:19*

NEW COVENANT REFERENCE

Jesus answered him, I have spoken openly to the world. I have always taught in a synagogue and in the temple [area], where the Jews [habitually] congregate (assemble); and I have spoken nothing secretly.
- *Yochanan (John) 18:20*

ISAIAH: Messiah's Passion (Atonement Sufferings)

I gave My back to the smiters and My cheeks to those who plucked off the hair; I hid not My face from shame and spitting. - *Isaiah 50:6*

NEW COVENANT REFERENCES

Then they spat in His face and struck Him with their fists; and some slapped Him in the face. - *Matthew 26:67*

And they spat on Him, and took the reed (staff) and struck Him on the head. - *Matthew 27:30*

So then Pilate took Jesus and scourged (flogged, whipped) Him. - *Yochanan (John) 19:1*

ISAIAH: Messiah Set His Face (with Determination)

For the Lord God helps Me; therefore have I not been ashamed or confounded. Therefore have I set My face like a flint, and I know that I shall not be put to shame. - *Isaiah 50:7*

NEW COVENANT REFERENCE

Now when the time was almost come for Jesus to be received up [to heaven], He steadfastly and determinedly set His face to go to Jerusalem. - *Luke 9:5*

ISAIAH: God's Salvation Revealed In Messiah Yeshua

The LORD has made bare His holy arm before the eyes of all the nations [revealing Himself as the One by Whose direction the redemption of Israel from captivity is accomplished], and all the ends of the earth shall witness the Salvation of our God. - *Isaiah 52:10*

Remember, the name 'Yeshua' means Salvation!

NEW COVENANT REFERENCES

[Simeon] took Him up in his arms and praised and thanked God and said,

And now, Lord, You are releasing Your servant to depart (leave this world) in peace, according to Your word.

For with my [own] eyes I have seen Your Salvation,

Which You have ordained and prepared before (in the presence of) all peoples,

A Light for revelation to the Gentiles [to disclose what was before un-known] and [to bring] praise and honor and glory to Your people Israel. *– Luke 2:28-32*

And all mankind shall see (behold and understand and at last acknowl-edge) the salvation of God (the deliverance from eternal death decreed by God). *– Luke 3:6*

ISAIAH: His Face Was Marred More than Any Man

[For many the Servant of God became an object of horror; many were astonished at Him.] His face and His whole appearance were marred more than any man's, and His form beyond that of the sons of men--but just as many were astonished at Him.

So shall He startle and sprinkle many nations, and kings shall shut their mouths because of Him;

For that which has not been told them shall they see, and that which they have not heard shall they consider and understand. - *Isaiah 52:14-15*

When Jesus was crucified, He had been beaten beyond recognition. The divine Blood that He shed was for the sprinkling of many nations, as the Blood of the Lamb of God Who takes away the sins of the world.

NEW COVENANT REFERENCES

For if [the mere] sprinkling of unholy and defiled persons with blood of goats and bulls and with the ashes of a burnt heifer is sufficient for the purification of the body,

How much more surely shall the blood of Christ, Who by virtue of [His] Spirit [His own preexistent divine personality] has offered Himself as an unblemished sacrifice to God, purify our consciences from dead works and lifeless observances to serve the [ever] living God?
- *Hebrews 9:13-14*

...As it is written, They shall see who have never been told of Him, and they shall understand who have never heard [of Him]. - *Romans 15:21*

ISAIAH: The Message, Who Would Believe It?

Who has believed (trusted in, relied upon, and clung to) our message [of that which was revealed to us]? And to whom has the arm of the Lord been disclosed? - *Isaiah 53:1*

NEW COVENANT REFERENCES

Even though He had done so many miracles before them (right before their eyes), yet they still did not trust in Him and failed to believe in Him--

So that what Isaiah the prophet said was fulfilled: Lord, who has believed our report and our message? And to whom has the arm (the power) of the Lord been shown (unveiled and revealed)? ...

Isaiah said this because he saw His glory and spoke of Him [Isa. 6:9-10]. - *Yochanan (John) 12:37-38, 41*

But they have not all heeded the Gospel; for Isaiah says, Lord, who has believed (had faith in) what he has heard from us?

So faith comes by hearing [what is told], and what is heard comes by the preaching [of the message that came from the lips] of Christ (the Messiah Himself). - *Romans 10:16-17*

ISAIAH: His Growth and Humility

For [the Servant of God] grew up before Him like a tender plant, and like a root out of dry ground; He has no form or comeliness [royal, kingly pomp], that we should look at Him, and no beauty that we should desire Him.

He was despised and rejected and forsaken by men, a Man of sorrows and pains, and acquainted with grief and sickness; and like One from Whom men hide their faces He was despised, and we did not appreciate His worth or have any esteem for Him. - *Isaiah 53:2-3*

God chose to send His Son, the Word made flesh, to be born in a stable, among the sheep.

Yeshua endured insults and persecutions; and finally, crucifixion to atone for mankind.

NEW COVENANT REFERENCE

And Jesus increased in wisdom (in broad and full understanding) and in stature and years, and in favor with God and man. - *Luke 2:52*

ISAIAH: His Healing Power

Surely He has borne our griefs (sicknesses, weaknesses, and distresses) and carried our sorrows and pains [of punishment], yet we [ignorantly] considered Him stricken, smitten, and afflicted by God [as if with leprosy]. - *Isaiah 53:4*

NEW COVENANT REFERENCES

When evening came, they brought to Him many who were under the power of demons, and He drove out the spirits with a word and restored to health all who were sick.

And thus He fulfilled what was spoken by the prophet Isaiah, He Himself took [in order to carry away] our weaknesses and infirmities and bore away our diseases. - *Matthew 8:16-17*

The same message which was proclaimed throughout all Judea, starting from Galilee after the baptism preached by John--

How God anointed and consecrated Jesus of Nazareth with the [Holy] Spirit and with strength and ability and power; how He went about doing good, in particular, curing all who were harassed and oppressed by [the power of] the devil, for God was with Him. - *Acts 10:37-38*

ISAIAH: His Atonement

But He was wounded for our transgressions, He was bruised for our guilt and iniquities; the chastisement [needful to obtain] peace and well-being for us was upon Him, and with the stripes [that wounded] Him we are healed and made whole.

All we like sheep have gone astray, we have turned every one to his own way; and the Lord has made to light upon Him the guilt and iniquity of us all. - *Isaiah 53:5-6*

The Salvation that Yeshua (Jesus) Messiah purchased for mankind was for the whole being - spirit, soul and body. He died for our sins; He died for us to be made whole.

NEW COVENANT REFERENCE

He was guilty of no sin, neither was deceit (guile) ever found on His lips...He personally bore our sins in His [own] body on the tree [as on an altar and offered Himself on it], that we might die (cease to exist) to sin and live to righteousness. By His wounds you have been healed.
- *I Peter 2:22-24*

ISAIAH: He Was Silent Before His Accusers

He was oppressed, [yet when] He was afflicted, He was submissive and opened not His mouth; like a lamb that is led to the slaughter, and as a sheep before her shearers is dumb, so He opened not His mouth. - *Isaiah 53:7*

NEW COVENANT REFERENCE

But when the charges were made against Him by the chief priests and elders, He made no answer. Then Pilate said to Him, Do You not hear how many and how serious are the things they are testifying against You? But He made no reply to him, not even to a single accusation, so that the governor marveled greatly. - *Matthew 27:12-14*

ISAIAH: He Had a Rich Man's Tomb

And they assigned Him a grave with the wicked, and with a rich man in His death, although He had done no violence, neither was any deceit in His mouth. - *Isaiah 53:9*

NEW COVENANT REFERENCES

When it was evening, there came a rich man from Arimathea, named Joseph, who also was a disciple of Jesus.

He went to Pilate and asked for the body of Jesus, and Pilate ordered that it be given to him.

And Joseph took the body and rolled it up in a clean linen cloth used for swathing dead bodies.

And laid it in his own fresh (undefiled) tomb, which he had hewn in the rock; and he rolled a big boulder over the door of the tomb and went away. - *Matthew 27:57-60*

Joseph, he of Arimathea, noble and honorable in rank and a respected member of the council (Sanhedrin), who was himself waiting for the kingdom of God, daring the consequences, took courage and ventured to go to Pilate and asked for the body of Jesus...

And Joseph bought a [fine] linen cloth [for swathing dead bodies], and, taking Him down from the cross, he rolled Him up in the [fine] linen cloth and placed Him in a tomb which had been hewn out of a rock. Then he rolled a [very large] stone against the door of the tomb. - *Mark 15:43, 46*

ISAIAH: His Resurrection on the Third Day

Yet it was the will of the Lord to bruise Him; He has put Him to grief and made Him sick. When You and He make His life an offering for sin [and He has risen from the dead, in time to come], He shall see His [spiritual] offspring. He shall prolong His days, and the will and pleasure of the Lord shall prosper in His hand. - *Isaiah 53:10*

NEW COVENANT REFERENCES

...This Fellow said, I am able to tear down the sanctuary of the temple of God and to build it up again in three days. - *Matthew 26:61*

But He had spoken of the temple which was His body. When therefore He had risen from the dead, His disciples remembered that He said this. And so they believed and trusted and relied on the Scripture and the word (message) Jesus had spoken. - *Yochanan (John) 2:21-22*

Jesus said to her, I am [Myself] the Resurrection and the Life. Whoever believes in (adheres to, trusts in, and relies on) Me, although he may die, yet he shall live; - *Yochanan (John) 11:25*

Then He [thoroughly] opened up their minds to understand the Scriptures, and said to them, Thus it is written that the Christ (the Messiah) should suffer and on the third day rise from (among) the dead. - *Luke 24:45-46*

The tombs were opened and many bodies of the saints who had fallen asleep in death were raised [to life]; And coming out of the tombs after His resurrection, they went into the holy city and appeared to many people. When the centurion and those who were with Him keeping watch over Jesus observed the earthquake and all that was happening, they were terribly frightened and filled with awe, and said, Truly this was God's Son! - *Matthew 27:50-54*

For I passed on to you first of all what I also had received, that Christ (the Messiah, the Anointed One) died for our sins in accordance with [what] the Scriptures [foretold],

That He was buried, that He arose on the third day as the Scriptures foretold. - *I Corinthians 15:3-4*

TANAKH REFERENCE

Come and let us return to the Lord, for He has torn so that He may heal us; He has stricken so that He may bind us up.

After two days He will revive us (quicken us, give us life); on the third day He will raise us up that we may live before Him. - *Hosea 6:2*

ISAIAH: He Was Counted Among the Transgressors

Therefore will I divide Him a portion with the great [kings and rulers], and He shall divide the spoil with the mighty, because He poured out His life unto death, and [He let Himself] be regarded as a criminal and be numbered with the transgressors; yet He bore [and took away] the sin of many and made intercession for the transgressors (the rebellious). - *Isaiah 53:12*

NEW COVENANT REFERENCES

And with Him they crucified two robbers, one on [His] right hand and one on His left. And the Scripture was fulfilled which says, He was counted among the transgressors. - *Mark 15:27-28*

For I tell you that this Scripture must yet be fulfilled in Me: And He was counted and classed among the wicked (the outlaws, the criminals); for what is written about Me has its fulfillment [has reached its end and is finally settled]. - *Luke 22:37*

Two others also, who were criminals, were led away to be executed with Him. - *Luke 23:32*

ISAIAH: Messiah as Teacher

And all your [spiritual] children shall be disciples [taught by the Lord and obedient to His will], and great shall be the peace and undisturbed composure of your children. - *Isaiah 54:13*

NEW COVENANT REFERENCE

It is written in [the book of] the Prophets, And they shall all be taught of God [have Him in person for their Teacher]. Everyone who has listened to and learned from the Father comes to Me. - *Yochanan (John) 6:4*

ISAIAH: The Deliverer Will Come from Zion

So [as the result of the Messiah's intervention] they shall [reverently] fear the name of the Lord from the west, and His glory from the rising of the sun. When the enemy shall come in like a flood, the Spirit of the Lord will lift up a standard against him and put him to flight [for He will come like a rushing stream which the breath of the Lord drives].

He shall come as a Redeemer to Zion and to those in Jacob (Israel) who turn from transgression, says the Lord. - *Isaiah 59:19-20*

NEW COVENANT REFERENCE

And so all Israel will be saved. As it is written, The Deliverer will come from Zion, He will banish ungodliness from Jacob. And this will be My covenant (My agreement) with them when I shall take away their sins. - *Romans 11:26-27*

Messiah Yeshua (Jesus) came to and out of Israel (Zion). The Word became flesh and dwelt among us! He came to save His people from their sins; to the Jew first, and also to the Gentile.

TANAKH REFERENCE

Oh, that the Salvation of Israel would come out of Zion! When the Lord shall restore the fortunes of His people, then Jacob shall rejoice and Israel shall be glad. - *Psalm 14:7*

It is interesting to note that this verse in Psalm 14 is number 7. Seven is God's biblical number for perfection and completion. Remember, Yeshua's name means "Salvation."

ISAIAH: The Spirit of the LORD God Is Upon Him

The Spirit of the Lord God is upon me, because the Lord has anointed and qualified me to preach the Gospel of good tidings to the meek, the poor, and afflicted; He has sent me to bind up and heal the brokenhearted, to proclaim liberty to the [physical and spiritual] captives and the opening of the prison and of the eyes to those who are bound. - *Isaiah 61:1*

NEW COVENANT REFERENCE

And He Himself conducted [a course of] teaching in their synagogues, being recognized and honored and praised by all.

So He came to Nazareth, [that Nazareth] where He had been brought up, and He entered the synagogue, as was His custom on the Sabbath day. And He stood up to read.

And there was handed to Him [the roll of] the book of the prophet Isaiah. He opened (unrolled) the book and found the place where it was written,

The Spirit of the Lord [is] upon Me, because He has anointed Me [the Anointed One, the Messiah] to preach the good news (the Gospel) to the poor; He has sent Me to announce release to the captives and recovery of sight to the blind, to send forth as delivered those who are oppressed [who are downtrodden, bruised, crushed, and broken down by calamity].

To proclaim the accepted and acceptable year of the Lord [the day when Salvation and the free favors of God profusely abound].

Then He rolled up the book and gave it back to the attendant and sat down; and the eyes of all in the synagogue were gazing [attentively] at Him.

And He began to speak to them: Today this Scripture has been fulfilled while you are present and hearing. - *Luke 4:15-21*

The word "Christ" in the original Greek of the Scriptures is "Christos". It is not a name, but rather, a title. It's meaning is "Anointed" and "Messiah."

JEREMIAH: A House of Prayer, Jesus Cleanses the Temple

Has this house, which is called by My Name, become a den of robbers in your eyes [a place of retreat for you between acts of violence]? Behold, I myself have seen it, says the Lord. - *Jeremiah 7:11*

NEW COVENANT REFERENCES

And Jesus went into the temple (whole temple enclosure) and drove out all who bought and sold in the sacred place, and He turned over the four-footed tables of the money changers and the chairs of those who sold doves.

He said to them, The Scripture says, My house shall be called a house of prayer; but you have made it a den of robbers. - *Matthew 21:12-13*

And they came to Jerusalem. And He went into the temple [area, the porches and courts] and began to drive out those who sold and bought in the temple area, and He overturned the [four-footed] tables of the money changers and the seats of those who dealt in doves...

And He taught and said to them, Is it not written, My house shall be called a house of prayer for all the nations? But you have turned it into a den of robbers. - *Mark 11:15, 17*

TANAKH REFERENCE

For My house shall be called a house of prayer for all nations. - *Isaiah 56:7*

JEREMIAH: A Righteous Branch, the Lord Our Righteousness

Behold, the days are coming, says the Lord, when I will raise up to David a righteous Branch (Sprout), and He will reign as King and do wisely and will execute justice and righteousness in the land.

In His days Judah shall be saved and Israel shall dwell safely; and this is His name by which He shall be called: The Lord Our Righteousness. - *Jeremiah 23:5-6*

In those days and at that time will I cause a righteous Branch [the Messiah] to grow up to David; and He shall execute justice and righteousness in the land.

In those days Judah shall be saved and Jerusalem shall dwell safely. And this is the name by which it will be called, The Lord is Our Righteousness (our Rightness, our Justice). - *Jeremiah 33:15-16*

NEW COVENANT REFERENCES

She will bear a Son, and you shall call His name Jesus [the Greek form of the Hebrew Joshua, which means Savior], For He will save His people from their sins [that is, prevent them from failing and missing the true end and scope of life, which is God]. - *Matthew 1:21*

Namely, the righteousness of God which comes by believing with personal trust and confident reliance on Jesus Christ (the Messiah). [And it is meant] for all who believe. For there is no distinction,

Since all have sinned and are falling short of the honor and glory which God bestows and receives.

[All] are justified and made upright and in right standing with God, freely and gratuitously by His grace (His unmerited favor and mercy), through the redemption which is [provided] in Christ Jesus. - *Romans 3:22-24*

And great and important and weighty, we confess, is the hidden truth (the mystic secret) of godliness. He [God] was made visible in human flesh, justified and vindicated in the [Holy] Spirit, was seen by angels, preached among the nations, believed on in the world, [and] taken up in glory. – *I Timothy 3:16*

JEREMIAH: King Herod's Decree

Thus says the Lord: A voice is heard in Ramah, lamentation and bitter weeping. Rachel is weeping for her children; she refuses to be comforted for her children, because they are no more. - *Jeremiah 31:15*

NEW COVENANT REFERENCE

Then Herod, when he realized that he had been misled by the wise men, was furiously enraged, and he sent and put to death all the male children in Bethlehem and in all that territory who were two years old and under, reckoning according to the date which he had investigated diligently and had learned exactly from the wise men.

Then was fulfilled what was spoken by the prophet Jeremiah: A voice was heard in Ramah, wailing and loud lamentation, Rachel weeping for her children; she refused to be comforted, because they were no more.

But when Herod died, behold, an angel of the Lord appeared in a dream to Joseph in Egypt and said, Rise, [tenderly] take unto you the Child and His mother and go to the land of Israel, for those who sought the Child's life are dead. - *Matthew 2:16-20*

105

EZEKIEL: Messiah, Our Shepherd and Davidic Descendent

And I will raise up over them one Shepherd and He shall feed them, even My Servant David; He shall feed them and He shall be their Shepherd.

And I the Lord will be their God and My Servant David a Prince among them; I the Lord have spoken it. - *Ezekiel 34:23-24*

NEW COVENANT REFERENCE

I am the Good Shepherd; and I know and recognize My own, and My own know and recognize Me.

Even as [truly as] the Father knows Me and I also know the Father--and I am giving My [very own] life and laying it down on behalf of the sheep.

And I have other sheep [beside these] that are not of this fold. I must bring and impel those also; and they will listen to My voice and heed My call, and so there will be [they will become] one flock under one Shepherd. - *Yochanan (John) 10:14-16*

TANAKH REFERENCE

The LORD is my Shepherd [to feed, guide, and shield me]. I shall not lack. - *Psalm 23:1*

It is interesting to note that the prophetic Scripture in Ezekiel 34 about our Shepherd is found in verse 23, as is Psalm 23 also about the Lord our Shepherd.

EZEKIEL: He Gives Us a New Heart, the New Birth Prophesied

A new heart will I give you and a new spirit will I put within you, and I will take away the stony heart out of your flesh and give you a heart of flesh.

And I will put my Spirit within you and cause you to walk in My statutes, and you shall heed My ordinances and do them. - *Ezekiel 36:26-27*

The Law was written by the finger of God upon stone tablets. The Word of God is written upon our hearts by the Holy Spirit.

NEW COVENANT REFERENCES

NOW THERE was a certain man among the Pharisees named Nicodemus, a ruler (a leader, an authority) among the Jews, who came to Jesus at night and said to Him, Rabbi, we know and are certain that You have come from God [as] a Teacher; for no one can do these signs (these wonderworks, these miracles--and produce the proofs) that You do unless God is with him. Jesus answered him, I assure you, most solemnly I tell you, that unless a person is born again (anew, from above), he cannot ever see (know, be acquainted with, and experience) the kingdom of God.

Nicodemus said to Him, How can a man be born when he is old? Can he enter his mother's womb again and be born? Jesus answered, I assure you, most solemnly I tell you, unless a man is born of water and [even] the Spirit, he cannot [ever] enter the kingdom of God. What is born of [from] the flesh is flesh [of the physical is physical]; and what is born of the Spirit is spirit. Marvel not [do not be surprised, astonished] at My telling you, You must all be born anew (from above). - *Yochanan (John) 3:1-7*

But to as many as did receive and welcome Him, He gave the authority (power, privilege, right) to become the children of God, that is, to those who believe in (adhere to, trust in, and rely on) His name. Who owe their birth neither to bloods nor to the will of the flesh [that of physical impulse] nor to the will of man [that of a natural father], but to God. [They are born of God!] - *Yochanan (John) 1:12-13*

DANIEL'S Prophecy of the Son of Man, Yeshua (Jesus)

I saw in the night visions, and behold, on the clouds of the heavens came One like a Son of man, and He came to the Ancient of Days and was presented before Him.

And there was given Him [the Messiah] dominion and glory and kingdom, that all peoples, nations, and languages should serve Him. His dominion is an everlasting dominion which shall not pass away, and His kingdom is one which shall not be destroyed. - *Daniel 7:13-14*

Daniel's prophecy is of the future coming of Yeshua (Jesus) Messiah (the Christ, the Anointed One). He shall not come to earth the second time as a baby. He shall come in the clouds with power and great glory.

NEW COVENANT REFERENCES

Then the sign of the Son of Man will appear in the sky, and then all the tribes of the earth will mourn and beat their breasts and lament in anguish, and they will see the Son of Man coming on the clouds of heaven with power and great glory [in brilliancy and splendor]. - *Matthew 24:30*

Jesus said to him, You have stated [the fact]. More than that, I tell you: You will in the future see the Son of Man seated at the right hand of the Almighty and coming on the clouds of the sky. - *Matthew 26:64*

Behold, He is coming with the clouds, and every eye will see Him, even those who pierced Him; and all the tribes of the earth shall gaze upon Him and beat their breasts and mourn and lament over Him. Even so [must it be]. Amen (so be it). - *Revelation 1:7*

HOSEA: Yahweh God Called His Son Out of Egypt

When Israel was a child, then I loved him and called My son out of Egypt. - *Hosea 11:1*

NEW COVENANT REFERENCE

Now after they (the wise men) had gone, behold, an angel of the Lord appeared to Joseph in a dream and said, Get up! [Tenderly] take unto you the young Child and His mother and flee to Egypt; and remain there till I tell you [otherwise], for Herod (the king of that day) intends to search for the Child in order to destroy Him.

And having risen, he took the Child and His mother by night and withdrew to Egypt

And remained there until Herod's death. This was to fulfill what the Lord had spoken by the prophet, Out of Egypt have I called My Son.
- *Matthew 2:13-15*

The name "Israel" means: He will rule (as) God.

The Sign of Jonah

Now the Lord had prepared and appointed a great fish to swallow up Jonah. And Jonah was in the belly of the fish three days and three nights. *- Jonah 1:17*

Then Jonah prayed to the Lord his God from the fish's belly, and said, I cried out of my distress to the Lord, and He heard me; out of the belly of Sheol cried I, and You heard my voice. For You cast me into the deep, into the heart of the seas, and the floods surrounded me; all Your waves and Your billows passed over me. Then I said, I have been cast out of Your presence and Your sight; yet I will look again toward Your holy temple. The waters compassed me about, even to [the extinction of] life; the abyss surrounded me, the seaweed was wrapped about my head. I went down to the bottoms and the very roots of the mountains; the earth with its bars closed behind me forever. Yet You have brought up my life from the pit and corruption, O Lord my God. *- Jonah 2:1-6*

NEW COVENANT REFERENCES

Then some of the scribes and Pharisees said to Him, Teacher, we desire to see a sign or miracle from You [proving that You are what You claim to be].

But He replied to them, an evil and adulterous generation (a generation morally unfaithful to God) seeks and demands a sign; but no sign shall be given to it except the sign of the prophet Jonah.

For even as Jonah was three days and three nights in the belly of the sea monster, so will the Son of Man be three days and three nights in the heart of the earth. - *Matthew 12:38-40*

The sign of Jonah, being three days and three nights in the belly of the whale was a prophetic signpost of Jesus being three days and three nights in the heart (core) of the earth. This is where He obtained the keys of death and Hades (Revelation 1:18). This is also where He preached to the spirits in prison (a holding place of the dead) to give them the Message of Salvation.

I Peter 3:19 - He preached to the spirits in prison

MICAH: Messiah's Birthplace

But you, Bethlehem Ephratah, you are little to be among the clans of Judah; [yet] out of you shall One come forth for Me Who is to be Ruler in Israel, Whose goings forth have been from of old, from ancient days (eternity). - *Micah 5:2*

The meaning of the prophet Micah's name is "Who is like the LORD?"

NEW COVENANT REFERENCES

And you Bethlehem, in the land of Judah, you are not in any way least or insignificant among the chief cities of Judah; for from you shall come a Ruler (Leader) Who will govern and shepherd My people Israel.
- *Matthew 2:6*

And Joseph also went up from Galilee from the town of Nazareth to Judea, to the town of David, which is called Bethlehem, because he was of the house and family of David, to be enrolled with Mary, his espoused (married) wife, who was about to become a mother. - *Luke 2:4-5*

For to you is born this day in the town of David a Savior, Who is Christ (the Messiah) the Lord! - *Luke 2:11*

Does not the Scripture tell us that the Christ (Messiah) will come from the offspring of David and from Bethlehem, the village where David lived? - *Yochanan (John) 7:42*

The name "Bethlehem" (Beit Lechem) in the Hebrew, means "House of Bread". Yeshua Messiah is the Living Bread that came down from Heaven. Not a physical nourishment, but a spiritual one.

I am the Living Bread which came down from Heaven; if any man eat of this bread, he shall live forever: and the bread that I will give is my flesh, which I will give for the life of the world. - *Yochanan (John) 6:51 KJV*

ZECHARIAH: Messiah, the Branch

Hear now, O Joshua the high priest, you and your colleagues who [usually] sit before you--for they are men who are a sign... [types of what is to come] --for behold, I will bring forth My servant the Branch.
- *Zechariah 3:8*

And say to him, Thus says the Lord of hosts: [You, Joshua] behold (look at, keep in sight, watch) the Man [the Messiah] whose name is the Branch, for He shall grow up in His place and He shall build the [true] temple of the Lord. - *Zechariah 6:12*

NEW COVENANT REFERENCE

He went and dwelt in a town called Nazareth, so that what was spoken through the prophets might be fulfilled: He shall be called a Nazarene [Branch, Separated One]. - *Matthew 2:23*

TANAKH REFERENCES

In that day the Branch of the Lord shall be beautiful and glorious, and the fruit of the land shall be excellent and lovely to those of Israel who have escaped. - *Isaiah 4:2*

Behold, the days are coming, says the Lord, when I will raise up to David a righteous Branch (Sprout), and He will reign as King and do wisely and will execute justice and righteousness in the land.

In His days Judah shall be saved and Israel shall dwell safely: and this is His name by which He shall be called: The Lord Our Righteousness. *– Jeremiah 23:5-6*

In those days and at that time will I cause a righteous Branch [the Messiah] to grow up to David; and He shall execute justice and righteousness in the land. *– Jeremiah 33:15*

Nazareth means "Branch" or "Separated One," as from the word Nazarite. Jesus was brought up in the town of Nazareth.

ZECHARIAH: Messiah's Inscription and Atonement in One Day

For behold, upon the stone which I have set before Joshua, upon that one stone are seven eyes or facets [the all-embracing providence of God and the seven-fold radiations of the Spirit of God]. Behold, I will carve upon it its inscription, says the Lord of hosts, and I will remove the iniquity and guilt of this land in a single day. - *Zechariah 3:9*

We have seen that Yeshua (Jesus) has been represented as the Stone (Isaiah 8:14, 28:16), that Joshua is the Hebrew representation of His Name (Salvation of the Lord), and that God's Spirit is Sevenfold (Isaiah 11:2). Now let us look at this multi-faceted passage as also containing prophecy of His atonement (removing iniquity in one day) and the mystery of His Inscription revealed in the B'rit Hadashah.

NEW COVENANT REFERENCES

And over His head they put the accusation against Him (the cause of His death), which read, This is Jesus, the King of the Jews. - *Matthew 27:37*

And it was the third hour (about nine o'clock in the morning) when they crucified Him. And the inscription of the accusation against Him was written above, The King of the Jews. - *Mark 15:26*

For there was also an inscription above Him in letters of Greek and Latin and Hebrew: This is the King of the Jews. - *Luke 23:38*

And Pilate also wrote a title (an inscription on a placard) and put it on the cross. And the writing was: Jesus the Nazarene, the King of the Jews. - *Yochanan (John) 19:19*

ZECHARIAH: He Rode Into Jerusalem on a Donkey

Rejoice greatly, O Daughter of Zion! Shout aloud, O Daughter of Jerusalem! Behold, your King comes to you; He is [uncompromisingly] just and having Salvation [triumphant and victorious], patient, meek, lowly, and riding on a donkey, upon a colt, the foal of a donkey. - *Zechariah 9:9*

NEW COVENANT REFERENCES

And when they came near Jerusalem and had reached Bethphage at the Mount of Olives, Jesus sent two disciples on ahead,

Saying to them, Go into the village that is opposite you, and at once you will find a donkey tied, and a colt with her; untie [them] and bring [them] to Me,

If anyone says anything to you, you shall reply, The Lord needs them, and he will let them go without delay.

This happened that what was spoken by the prophet might be fulfilled, saying,

Say to the Daughter of Zion [inhabitants of Jerusalem], Behold, your King is coming to you, lowly and riding on a donkey, and on a colt, the foal of a donkey. - *Matthew 21:1-5*

And Jesus, having found a young donkey, rode upon it [just] as it is written in the Scriptures,

Do not fear, O Daughter of Zion! Look! Your King is coming, sitting on a donkey's colt! - *Yochanan (John) 12:14-15*

ZECHARIAH: He was Pierced

And I will pour out upon the house of David and upon the inhabitants of Jerusalem the Spirit of grace or unmerited favor and supplication.

And they shall look [earnestly] upon Me Whom they have pierced, and they shall mourn for Him as one mourns for his only son, and shall be in bitterness for Him as one who is in bitterness for his firstborn.
- *Zechariah 12:10*

NEW COVENANT REFERENCES

But one of the soldiers pierced His side with a spear, and immediately Blood and water came (flowed) out.

And he who saw it (the eyewitness) gives this evidence, and his testimony is true; and he knows that he tells the truth, that you may believe also...

And again another Scripture says, They shall look on Him Whom they have pierced. - *Yochanan (John) 19:34-35, 37*

Behold, He is coming with the clouds, and every eye will see Him, even those who pierced Him; and all the tribes of the earth shall gaze upon Him and beat their breasts and mourn and lament over Him. Even so [must it be]. Amen (so be it). - *Revelation 1:7*

ZECHARIAH: Wounded in the House of His Friends

And one shall say to him, What are these wounds on your breast or between your hands? Then he will answer, Those with which I was wounded [when disciplined] in the house of my [loving] friends. - *Zechariah 13:6*

NEW COVENANT REFERENCE

So the other disciples kept telling him, We have seen the Lord! But he said to them, Unless I see in His hands the marks made by the nails and put my finger into the nail prints, and put my hand into His side, I will never believe [it].

Eight days later His disciples were again in the house, and Thomas was with them. Jesus came, though they were behind closed doors, and stood among them and said, Peace to you!

Then He said to Thomas, Reach out your finger here, and see My hands; and put out your hand and place [it] in My side. Do not be faithless and incredulous, but [stop your unbelief and] believe!

Thomas answered Him, My Lord and my God! - *Yochanan (John) 20:25-28*

ZECHARIAH: Smite the Shepherd, Sheep Scattered

Awake, O sword, against My shepherd and against the man who is My associate, says the Lord of hosts; smite the shepherd and the sheep [of the flock] shall be scattered, and I will turn back My hand and stretch it out again upon the little ones [of the flock]. - *Zechariah 13:7*

NEW COVENANT REFERENCES

Then Jesus said to them, You will all be offended and stumble and fall away because of Me this night [distrusting and deserting Me], for it is written, I will strike the Shepherd, and the sheep of the flock will be scattered.

But after I am raised up [to life again], I will go ahead of you to Galilee. - *Matthew 26:31-32*

And Jesus said to them, You will all fall away this night [that is, you will be caused to stumble and will begin to distrust and desert Me], for it stands written, I will strike the Shepherd, and the sheep will be scattered. - *Mark 14:27*

MALACHI: Messiah Had a Forerunner

BEHOLD, I send My messenger, and he shall prepare the way before Me. And the Lord [the Messiah], Whom you seek, will suddenly come to His temple; the Messenger or Angel of the covenant, Whom you desire, behold, He shall come, says the Lord of hosts. - *Malachi 3:1*

Behold, I will send you Elijah the prophet before the great and terrible day of the Lord comes. - *Malachi 4:5*

Yeshua Messiah's forerunner was John the Baptist and their mothers were cousins. Elizabeth, John's mother, was past the age of childbearing. God gave her and husband Zachariah a miracle.

NEW COVENANT REFERENCES

In those days there appeared John the Baptist, preaching in the Wilderness (Desert) of Judea and saying, Repent (think differently; change your mind, regretting your sins and changing your conduct), for the kingdom of heaven is at hand.

This is he who was mentioned by the prophet Isaiah when he said, The voice of one crying in the wilderness (shouting in the desert), Prepare the road for the Lord, make His highways straight (level, direct). [Isaiah 40:3] - *Matthew 3:1-3*

This is the one of whom it is written, Behold, I send My messenger ahead of You, who shall make ready Your way before You.

And if you are willing to receive and accept it, John himself is Elijah who was to come [before the kingdom]. - *Matthew 11:10, 14*

The disciples asked Him, then why do the scribes say that Elijah must come first?

He replied, Elijah does come and will get everything restored and ready. But I tell you that Elijah has come already, and they did not know or recognize him, but did to him as they liked. So also the Son of Man is going to be treated and suffer at their hands. Then the disciples understood that He spoke to them about John the Baptist. - *Matthew 17:10-13*

THE BEGINNING [of the facts] of the good news (the Gospel) of Jesus Christ, the Son of God. Just as it is written in the prophet Isaiah: Behold, I send My messenger before Your face, who will make ready Your way. A voice of one crying in the wilderness [shouting in the desert], Prepare the way of the Lord, make His beaten tracks straight (level and passable)! - *Mark 1:1-3*

But the angel said to him, Do not be afraid, Zachariah, because your petition was heard, and your wife Elizabeth will bear you a son, and you must call his name John [God is favorable]. - *Luke 1:13*

And you, little one, shall be called a prophet of the Most High; for you shall go on before the face of the Lord to make ready His ways.
- *Luke 1:76*

There came a man sent from God whose name was John. This man came to witness, that he might testify of the Light, that all men might believe in it [adhere to it, trust it, and rely upon it] through him. - *Yochanan (John) 1:6-7*

He said, I am the voice of one crying aloud in the wilderness [the voice of one shouting in the desert], Prepare the way of the Lord [level, straighten out, the path of the Lord], as the prophet Isaiah said. - *Yochanan (John) 1:23*

TANAKH REFERENCE

A voice of one who cries: Prepare in the wilderness the way of the Lord [clear away the obstacles]; make straight and smooth in the desert a highway for our God!

Every valley shall be lifted and filled up, and every mountain and hill shall be made low; and the crooked and uneven shall be made straight and level, and the rough places a plain.

And the glory and (majesty and splendor) of the Lord shall be revealed, and all flesh shall see it together; for the mouth of the Lord has spoken it. - *Isaiah 40:3-5*

MALACHI: The Sun of Righteousness, Healing in His Wings

But unto you who revere and worshipfully fear My Name shall the Sun of Righteousness arise with healing in His wings and His beams, and you shall go forth and gambol like calves [released] from the stall and leap for joy. - *Malachi 4:2*

The word "wings" in the Hebrew is "kanaph" and it means an edge or extremity; (specifically of a bird or army) a wing, (of a garment or bed-clothing). In one of the references below you will see a B'rit Hadashah reference to a daughter of Abraham being healed by touching the hem of Yeshua's (Jesus') garment.

NEW COVENANT REFERENCES

And behold, a woman who had suffered from a flow of blood for twelve years came up behind Him and touched the fringe of His garment;

For she kept saying to herself, If I only touch His garment, I shall be restored to health.

And Jesus turned around and, seeing her, He said, Take courage, daughter! Your faith has made you well. And at once the woman was restored to health. - *Matthew 9:20-22*

And those in the boat knelt and worshiped Him, saying, Truly You are the Son of God!

And when they had crossed over to the other side, they were ashore at Gennesaret.

And when the men of that place recognized Him, they sent around into all the surrounding country and brought to Him all who were sick

And begged Him to let them merely touch the fringe of His garment; and as many as touched it were perfectly restored. - *Matthew 14:33-36*

To bring and give the knowledge of Salvation to His people in the forgiveness and remission of their sins. Because of and through the heart of tender mercy and loving-kindness of our God, a Light from on high will dawn upon us and visit [us]. - *Luke 1:77-78*

God's Word is Perfect: Messiah Yeshua, His Cross and Twenty Two (22)

There are eight places (eight is the Biblical number of covenant) in the Word of God all contained in chapters numbered twenty-two (22) that are profoundly messianic, with four in the Tanakh being prophetic-messianic:

Genesis 22 - Where Isaac was offered to God as a sacrifice at His request and a ram was provided as a substitute.

2 Samuel 22 - Which is a chapter devoted in praise to the Lord God for deliverance, Salvation and overcoming through Him.

1 Chronicles 22 - The materials listed used in building the tabernacle of the Lord are symbolic of the Cross - iron for nails, cedar for wood. Stones and bronze are messianic symbols, as Jesus is the stone that the builders rejected and the Chief Cornerstone; His feet glowed liked burnished (bright) bronze in Revelation 1:15.

Psalm 22 - This Psalm is the most messianic prophetic writing in the Tanakh as a picture of the crucifixion.

Isaiah 22:22 - Is pinnacle, as a verse speaking of Messiah Yeshua as the "key of David".

Matthew 22 - Where Yeshua gave a parable of the kingdom of Heaven being like a King who gave a wedding banquet for His Son.

Luke 22 - This chapter occurred on the Passover when Yeshua and His disciples partook of the last supper. He quoted from Isaiah 53:12. He prayed in the garden of Gethsemane (meaning "olive press"), was arrested and quoted Psalm 110:1 during questioning. Jesus revealed Himself as I AM.

Revelation 22 - This is the last chapter in the B'rit Hadashah of God's Word and contains precious words from our Lord Jesus Christ (the Messiah).

The Almighty God is perfect, Holy, and He is a God of plan, purpose, design and order. Two plus two equals four (2+2=4). When you look at the Cross, it points in four directions, up (North), down (South), to the right (East) and to the left (West). He died for all mankind to be saved, to the four corners of the earth. He died for every tribe and nation. His Salvation reaches out to the ends of the earth and it is for all peoples. This is our God; perfect Love.

The Amazing Verse 33 Scriptures, 12 in B'rit Hadashah

Yeshua (Jesus) laid down His life in the crucifixion at age thirty-three (33). It is interesting to note the following Scriptures (thus displaying the divine perfection of God's Holy Word):

And when they came to a place called Golgotha [Latin: Calvary], which means The Place of a Skull. - *Matthew 27:33 (this is where He was crucified)*

[Saying], Behold, we are going up to Jerusalem, and the Son of Man will be turned over to the chief priests and the scribes; and they will condemn and sentence Him to death and turn Him over to the Gentiles. - *Mark 10:33*

And He took with Him Peter and James and John, and began to be struck with terror and amazement and deeply troubled and depressed. - *Mark 14:33 (in the Garden Gethsemane before His arrest & crucifixion).*

And when the sixth hour (about midday) had come, there was darkness over the whole land until the ninth hour (about three o'clock). - *Mark 15:33 (on the cross just before He died)*

Nevertheless, I must continue on My way today and tomorrow and the day after that--- for it will never do for a prophet to be destroyed away from Jerusalem! - *Luke 13:33 (Jesus prophesying of His death)*

They will flog Him and kill Him; and on the third day He will rise again. - *Luke 18:33*

And [Simon Peter] said to Him, Lord, I am ready to go with You both to prison and to death. - *Luke 22:33*

And when they came to the place which is called The Skull [Latin: Calvary; Hebrew: Golgotha], there they crucified Him, and [along with] the criminals, one on the right and one on the left. - *Luke 23:33*

Therefore Jesus said, For a little while I am [still] with you, and then I go back to Him Who sent Me. - *Yochanan (John) 7:33*

He said this to signify in what manner He would die. - *Yochanan (John) 12:33*

[Dear] little children, I am to be with you only a little longer. You will look for Me and, as I told the Jews, so I tell you now: you are not able to come where I am going. - *Yochanan (John) 13:33*

But when they came to Jesus and they saw that He was already dead, they did not break His legs. - *Yochanan (John) 19:33*

Yeshua (Jesus) laid down His life for us at age 33. The word Salvation is found in thirty three (33) verses in the Prophets (kjv): twenty-six (26) times in Isaiah and seven (7) times in the rest of the Prophets:

Isaiah 12:2, 12:3, 17:10, 25:9, 26:1, 33:2, 33:6, 45:8, 45:17, 46:13, 49:6, 49:8, 51:5, 51:6, 51:8, 52:7, 52:10, 56:1, 59:11, 59:16, 59:17, 60:18, 61:10, 62:1, 62:11 and 63:5.

Jeremiah 3:23, Jonah 2:9, Micah 7:7, Habakkuk 3:8, 3:13, 3:18 and Zechariah 9:9.

A PRAYER

"And He said to them, These are the words which I spoke to you, while I was yet with you, that all things must be fulfilled, which were written in the law of Moses, and in the prophets, and in the psalms, concerning Me." - *(Yeshua) JESUS*

And He opened their understanding, that they might comprehend the Scriptures. - *Luke 24:44-45*

Prayer to receive Yeshua (Jesus) as Savior:

Dear Lord God,

I come to You today and thank You for sending Your Son Yeshua (Jesus Christ) Messiah to die for my sins. Lord Jesus, I believe in You, and I receive You today as my Beloved Messiah and Savior. Wash me in Your precious atoning Blood that cleanses from all sin.

Fill me with Your precious Ruach Ha' Kodesh (Holy Spirit); in Yeshua's (Jesus') Name, Amen - so be it.

_____   _____

your name and date

"…for it is the Blood that makes atonement for the soul."

- Leviticus 17:11 NKJV

"…Behold the Lamb of God, Who takes away the sin of the world."

- John 1:29 NKJV

"And I saw no temple therein: for the Lord God Almighty and the Lamb are the Temple of it."

- Revelation 21:22 KJV

ENDNOTES

1. The New Strong's Exhaustive Concordance of the Bible, copyright 1995 by Thomas Nelson Publishers

2. The "Parable" of Light - Derek Prince Ministries - Jerusalem, Israel (online)

3. The Prophecy Bible, copyright 2002 by Morris Cerullo World Evangelism, Page 15

4. The New Strong's Exhaustive Concordance of the Bible, copyright 1995 by Thomas Nelson Publishers

ABOUT THE AUTHOR

Dr. Janiel Guthrie grew up on a farm and gave her life to her Lord and Savior, Jesus Christ at a young age. She has a love for and insight into the Scriptures that can only be by the hand of providence.

Dr. Guthrie's passion is to do the will of God and see His purposes manifest on the earth in the lives of others. Janiel (jay-nee-el) is also a worship singer with a prophetic psalmist gifting.

Made in the USA
Charleston, SC
29 January 2013